Easy Like
Sunday Mourning

Jennie Marts

For: Linda

Always Believe in
Your Dreams!

Jennie
Marts

THIS BOOK IS DEDICATED TO

Todd, Tyler and Nick

The keepers of my heart

You have my love for now and always

Believe

PROL🐾GUE

If Jim Edwards had only known that today really was the last day of the rest of his life, he definitely would have spent it better. He would have stopped at Starbucks on his way to work for a latte instead of being on his sixth cup of awful office coffee. He'd have gone out to lunch and enjoyed some of the late-summer sunshine instead of absently eating a bologna sandwich while he worked at this desk. He'd have left work early instead of still being hunched over his computer at eleven o'clock on a Saturday night. He would have taken Charlotte Foster out to dinner, somewhere nice, maybe even to a movie where they could have held hands in the dark. And he would have chosen today as the day to finally tell her that he loved her.

Instead, he had stayed at the office, lost in the world of software and codes, methodically plodding away at the new program he had been working on with his boss, Jeremy Rogers. He had been with Jeremy's video game production company for two years and was excited about the latest game they were working on. With its new AI capabilities and revolutionary character building, it was bound to change the future of gaming forever.

Unfortunately, Jim's part in this game was over, as his dead body currently lay slumped atop his desk. Dark coffee from his overturned cup lay pooled on his desktop, soaking into his ergonomically correct mouse pad, and his head lay across his now silent keyboard. The spacebar pushed his mouth into a macabre death grin as the green light from the computer screen, bearing the logo of Rogers' Realms, reflected off his balding forehead.

Gravel crunched under the tires of the SUV as Maggie, Jeremy, and the boys pulled up to the cabin in the woods. From the passenger seat, Maggie gazed at the charming setting—the rustic little log cabin set against the backdrop of the Rocky Mountains—and hoped the spider crawling across her new hiking boot wasn't an indication of how the day was going to go.

She kicked the spider off and crushed it with the toe of her shoe, then looked across to the man sitting in the driver's seat.

Jeremy grinned. "I'm so glad you came up here with me. I can't wait to show you my cabin." He wiggled his eyebrows at her. "You ready for an adventure?"

Good question. Was she really ready for an adventure? Not just for a day in the mountains, but for this new adventure in her life called dating. A year and a half ago, her world had been turned upside down when Chad, her husband of eighteen years, walked into their bedroom and told her he was leaving her for a waitress he had met at Hooters. Hooters! Maggie had a law degree, and he preferred to converse with a woman whose wardrobe included scrunchy socks and shiny orange booty shorts.

In under ten minutes, he had shattered her world as she knew it and left a huge, gaping hole where her heart had been. She'd tried dating a few times, but evidently the anger and bitterness she carried toward men didn't make her a very good companion. Until Jeremy.

They'd met this summer, and his kindness and attention had begun to chip away at some of the hard edges of the wall she had built around her heart. She found herself letting him in, one step at a time, then fear and distrust would slam another door closed, and she would retreat into a dark, locked room of solitude and pain. But he hadn't given up. Every time she shut a door, he showed up at a window, shining a flashlight into her darkness and inviting her back into life.

She looked at him now as he unfolded his tall frame from the seat and stood to stretch. His dark hair flopped across his eyes, and he pushed his black-framed glasses back up his nose. He was the quintessential nerd who grew into his looks and didn't realize how handsome he was.

He leaned into the car, his eagerness to show her around evident by the huge grin on his face. "You ready?"

His smile and enthusiasm were infectious, and Maggie nodded. "Ready as I'll ever be."

She opened the car door and inhaled the crisp mountain air. It was late summer, and the sun shone through the aspen trees, a few of the leaves already turning yellow in anticipation of fall.

The scent of pine trees and wildflowers filled the air, and for the first time, she felt as if she might actually *be* ready. Ready to step out of the dark shroud she had pulled around herself and to take a chance on this new man. She smiled at the thought that Jeremy would actually appreciate the symbolism of a dark shroud due to his love of all things *Star Wars*.

The back doors of the SUV opened, and her two sons tumbled out. The sight of her oldest son, Drew, stepping from the truck caught her off guard. At seventeen, and a recent graduate, he was on the cusp of becoming a man. She still wasn't used to the whiskers evident on his chin, and his going to college in less than a month was one more new adventure she would have to face.

Chad had walked out on not only her but their two sons, and the boys had become fiercely protective of her, forming a tight unit of their small family. Drew had taken on the role of the man of the house and bonded with Maggie over taking extra care to safeguard the emotional well-being of his fourteen-year old brother, Dylan.

Drew looked at her, and they shared a smile as they watched Dylan run around the cabin, proclaiming everything to be "cool" and "so awesome."

As protective as they were, both boys had bonded with Jeremy over the last few months. He originally sparked their interest by telling them his company had designed their favorite video game, *Call to Action,* but had won them over with his easy laughter and all around nice-guy-ness. He was a big kid at heart and would spend hours playing video games with them, teaching them strategies and giving them inside tips on the game. Treating them as his buddies, he often brought over pizza and Skittles—not as a way to buy their affection, but as a nice gesture, and because he loved Skittles.

He had easily won over the kids, but Maggie's heart needed more than pizza and rainbow-colored candies.

Jeremy came around the car and took her hand. "You look amazing, by the way. Not that you don't look awesome in your courtroom power suits and heels, but I like this outdoorsy look of you all decked out in hiking boots and shorts." He leaned down and nuzzled her neck. "And you smell good. Is that a new perfume?"

Maggie laughed. "Yes, it's called bug repellent. And I'm still not sure about these hiking boots. They make my feet look ginormous." She looked down at her outfit. She had been blessed with great metabolism. Her figure was tall and slim, so she could get away with most clothing choices, but being tall came with big feet, and the boots felt heavy and awkward. For what they cost, they should have made her feet look small and come with solid gold laces.

She had made a mad dash to their local outdoor store the night before to purchase the expensive boots and spent another hundred dollars on this outfit and what she deemed outdoor necessities. The khaki shorts and light blue V-neck Henley were comfortable and boasted of quick-drying material and UV protection. The bug spray, two-pound bag of trail mix, and bird-watching guidebook may have been overkill, but she was in a hurry and wanted to be prepared.

"Well, I think you look great. I'm still amazed that a hottie like you is interested in a dork like me. But I'm not complaining." Jeremy laughed and pulled her toward the cabin.

He called for the boys and gave them all a tour of the little log building, which had been in his family for years. The cabin was set against the side of the mountain, a rock chimney climbing up one side and blue-and-white-checked curtains in the windows.

Opening the door, Maggie was enchanted by the big stone fireplace and thick throw rugs on the wood plank floor. Rocking chairs and cozy throws sat around the fireplace, ready to be snuggled into and curled under. The cabin smelled like pine and a mixture of cinnamon and vanilla. "What time do the seven dwarves get back? I want to make sure to have the dishes sparkling and their supper on the table."

"You don't have to make them supper, Mom," Drew said, stepping into the cabin and lugging a big tub of food from the car. "You brought enough trail mix to feed them for days."

Maggie grinned sheepishly. In truth, she didn't really even like trail mix. It was like having M&M's, but with obstacles.

Dylan raced in behind his older brother, grabbing for the giant bag of granola. "I love trail mix. And I love this place. It's awesome."

Jeremy looked like he would burst from happiness. "I knew you'd love it! Isn't it so great? Snide fairy-tale comments aside, there are a few things you should know." He pointed at the light fixtures on the ceiling. "We have electricity but no running water. This place is rustic."

"No running water?" Maggie asked in dismay. "What about the ladies' room?"

He pointed out the window to a set of steps carved into the mountain that led up to a small building painted a sunny yellow. "We call that Tinkle House. You might have to share it with a spider or two, but it's stocked with toilet paper, and it gets the job done."

Maggie shuddered at the thought of sharing her personal space with a spider. Or two. She figured she could just hold it.

Jeremy clapped his hands together. In the few months they'd been dating, she'd yet to see Jeremy in a bad mood, but coming to the cabin today had him simply delirious with joy. "Who's ready for a brisk hike before we eat lunch?"

Drew shrugged, but Dylan dropped the bag of trail mix, jumping to his feet in excitement. "I'll go."

Maggie shook her head. "Count me out for this one. I have a little work to finish before I can thoroughly enjoy my day. You guys go on ahead. I'll stay here and get my case file finished and be ready to roast hot dogs by the time you get back."

In truth, she did have work to do, but she was also glad to give Jeremy time to spend alone with the boys. They needed more male bonding in their lives and going for a hike in the mountains would give them time to spit and burp and kick rocks and do whatever other manly things men did in the mountains.

Jeremy looked a little disappointed, but he quickly rallied as Dylan asked him a question about deer tracks, and Maggie's heart filled to see her son get so excited. She had a feeling the tall, cute, nerdy guy who claimed he was her "boyfriend" had something to do with her heart filling as well—but for now, she was giving Dylan the credit.

Smiling, Maggie watched her sons take off up the trail with her "boyfriend." She sighed and did a mental eye roll. She was thirty-nine years old and using the term "boyfriend." It felt so juvenile, like she was back in high school and trying for the affection of the cute football player. But in her case, she had tried the football player, and that hadn't work out so great. She was now trying to win over the cute, nerdy guy with the glasses who was the president of the Math Club and understood physics. She sighed and headed to the car for her briefcase.

Almost an hour later, she had finished the case files, but her plan of "holding it" was not working. She pushed a lock of her long, dark hair behind her ear and blew her bangs out of her eyes as she climbed the steps to the little yellow building with the half-moon crescent cut out of the front of the door.

Reaching the top of the stairs, she hesitantly entered the little outhouse and after checking for spiders and snakes, she quickly took care of her business.

Maggie pushed open the door, preparing to take a deep breath of fresh air, but instead let out a screech of terror. Scrambling back into the outhouse, she yanked the door shut behind her. Her breath came in quick puffs. She looked out the little window in the door and there, sitting in the path, effectively blocking her exit, sat a large brown bear.

Maggie pulled her phone from her pocket and speed-dialed Jeremy's number.

"Hey, you," Jeremy's voice sounded through the phone. "Did you miss me already?" She heard him chuckle softly.

"I'm in the outhouse," she screamed into the phone. "And there's a bear outside! Come back and help me!"

"What? I told you...reception's terrible...here. What did...say? Something...your hair?"

"Not my hair!" she shrieked in frustration. "A bear! A bear! I'm trapped in the outhouse!"

"A bear...outhouse?"

"What's going on?" Maggie could hear Drew's voice. She could hear snippets of the men talking to each other in the background.

"I couldn't really hear her... reception's spotty up here...she was kind of shrieking..." Jeremy told her sons.

"My mom doesn't really shriek," she heard Dylan reply.

"I think...said there's a bear trapped in the outhouse," Jeremy said.

Maggie groaned.

Her frustration grew worse as she heard Dylan's voice take on an excited tone. "Cool, let's go."

No. Not cool. Definitely not cool. "Jeremy, get back here. Please."

A large thud slammed against the outhouse door. Maggie screamed. The bear's snout poked into the half-moon window. He seemed to be sniffing out this weird animal with the expensive perfume.

A puff of hot, moist air came through the window and bear spittle landed on Maggie's arm. She screamed again, and the phone flew from her hands.

"No! No! Nooo!" She scrambled to catch it before it hit the side of the shelf and dropped into the one-seater.

Helplessly, she looked into the murky depths of the hole and croaked, "Can you hear me now?"

The bear scratched his large paw down the front of the door. She jumped and screamed once more. He was up on his back legs, his big head obscuring the little window, as he curiously looked inside.

"Okay, this is ridiculous," she said out loud. "I am a highly paid, professional lawyer. I deal with drug dealers and criminals every day. I am a mother of teenage boys. I have a college degree. How hard can it be to deal with a bear?"

She continued her litany of self-talk as she scanned the little house for a weapon. The walls were painted a cheery yellow, and a blue and yellow braided rug lay on the floor. A magazine holder was affixed to the wall, and Maggie gawked in amazement at the *Better Homes and Gardens* that was dated July 17, 1968. The pages were curled and yellowed with age, but otherwise the magazine was still in pristine condition. However, unless she was going to read him recipes and tips on how to be a sixties housewife, the magazines were not going to help her with the bear.

In one corner of the outhouse sat a tall toilet paper holder, handcrafted from old coffee cans and flowered contact paper. A framed picture of an outhouse hung on the wall, rounding out her arsenal of weapons. Well, she was nothing if not resourceful.

Minutes later, a trickle of sweat ran down the side of her face as Maggie carefully scooted forward to peer out the tiny window. The bear's head had disappeared from view, and Maggie silently prayed that the beast had lumbered off so she could escape the hot, stuffy little building.

Cautiously easing the door open a crack, she saw today was not the day her prayers would be answered. She simultaneously launched both rolls at the bear while she screamed, "Go on!" then slammed the door shut again.

She cautiously looked out the window, hoping to see a bear-free path, but the big beast still sat there, completely unfazed by the launched Charmin missiles that had failed to land anywhere near his hulking body. Maggie groaned as she saw the white roll stuck in a bush, a foot of loose end waving in the breeze as if in white-flag surrender.

"Okay, you can do this. I am woman, hear me roar!" She began her self-talk again as she tried to think of how to get herself out of this predicament. She leaned against the wall and untied her expensive hiking boots. They would be worth the hundred dollars if they could get rid of this bear. She had spent sixty dollars on the shirt she was wearing. It deflected harmful UV rays and had built-in insect repellant. She warily thought she should have looked harder to find the shirt that had wildlife repellant. Who cared about a little mosquito when she was trying to ward off a bear?

The door creaked as Maggie eased it open once again. She took a deep breath and tried not to rush her attack this time. She wanted to scare it off, not make it angry. The bear sat about six feet away, in the middle of the path, eyeing her curiously as it licked its giant paw.

It used its teeth to dig at something between his claws, and Maggie took aim and threw her hiking boot at her furry foe. The boot thudded against the bear's large haunch, and he grunted and shifted his weight.

"No," Maggie cried in defeat, a tear threatening to spill from her eye. She shook her head and drew herself up to her full height of five feet, nine inches (now in her sock feet), and she clutched the second boot tighter in her hand.

"You can do this. You can do this." She drew her arm back, ready for the next shoe launch.

"Hey, bear," she yelled. "You're not so tough. Go on! Get out of here! Go find some honey!"

The bear just looked at her, impervious to her taunts.

She drew her arm back. With all her might, she threw the boot at the bear, simultaneously letting loose a ferocious tribal yell.

She watched the hiking boot sail through the air and land with a dull thump right on the bear's snout. Her fierce tribal yell turned into a high-pitched girlish shriek as the bear let out an annoyed grunt, and she pulled the door to the outhouse shut and threw the lock.

Outside, she heard the bear moving toward the door, then a group of excited hoots and hollers. Through the tiny window, she heard a cacophony of pots and pans being banged together from the cabin below, and she recognized the hollering of Jeremy and her boys.

"Hey, I'm in here," she yelled out the little window. "Help!"

"We got you, Mom," she heard Drew yell. She sank to the floor of the outhouse in relief, her worries about spiders now forgotten.

A few minutes later the door rattled, and she screamed again.

"It's me, Jeremy. Unlock the door."

"Is the bear gone?" she yelled back.

"No, we're sitting out here sharing a picnic basket with it."

"Not funny."

"Yes, it's gone," he said. "Unlock the door."

She pulled the latch back and cautiously eased the door open. Poking her head out, she looked around for the bear before throwing herself into Jeremy's arms. Overcome with relief, she reached an arm out and pulled her two sons into a group hug.

Dylan's eyes were bright with excitement. "That was so cool, Mom! Did you see how cool that bear was?"

She lifted her head from Jeremy's neck and looked around the forest. "Where did it go? Are you sure it's gone?"

"Yes," Jeremy said. "It lumbered off up the side of the mountain. The racket we were making must have annoyed it enough to make it take off."

The gravel of the path dug into her socked feet, but she didn't release her grip around Jeremy. "Thanks for saving me. I accidentally dropped my cell phone down the hole."

Jeremy peeked into the outhouse. "Do you want me to fish it out?"

"Nope. Not even a little."

Half an hour later, she sat in the cabin, a cup of hot tea in her hands, and listened to the boys retell the bear tale a third time, the bear getting bigger with each version.

"Only my mom would think to launch a toilet paper grenade at a bear," Drew said, holding his side from another round of laughter.

"Maybe the bear had to go," Dylan said, then cracked himself up in true fourteen-year-old form.

Jeremy ducked his head slightly as he came through the cabin door, a flannel shirt held loosely in his hand. He sat on the sofa next to Maggie and wrapped a long arm around her shoulder as he set the red plaid shirt in her lap.

He looked sideways at her from below the lock of dark bangs that constantly fell into his eyes and squeezed her shoulder. "You sure you're okay? I brought you a shirt in case you were cold. I would offer you my jacket, but you absconded with it last week, and I have yet to get it back."

Maggie had pilfered his coat during their date the weekend before. She had acted like she was cold, but she really just loved the jacket. It was soft black leather and custom-made for Jeremy. A large emblem of his favorite video game, *World of Warcraft*, was embroidered onto the back, the vibrant threads of color standing out against the black fabric.

It was also her favorite, and she and Jeremy had originally met each other in the online world of the game. *World of Warcraft* had been her secret obsession for the past year, a fantasy world of dwarves and raids and a great release from the drama and stress of the courtroom. She had stumbled onto it by accident, then found she looked forward to her evenings shut up in her office, fighting dragons and mystical beasts. Embarrassed by the fact that she was playing a fantasy game loved by teenagers, she kept her game-playing habits a secret.

She had met Jeremy in person when he arrived to pick up her friend, Sunny, for a blind date. He was taking Sunny on a surprise date to play *World of Warcraft*. The surprise was on him, though, when it turned out she was terrible at the game. Left alone for a few minutes before the date, Maggie and Jeremy's conversation had turned to the game, and somehow she found herself spilling her secret obsession to him. They realized they had been playing in the same group for months and knew each other through their online characters.

After it was clear that he and Sunny weren't a match, he had approached Maggie in the game and in true nerd form—had his character ask hers for her number. He and Maggie had continued to play almost nightly, but now they were on the same team.

She had nabbed the coat last weekend and loved the jacket because of the symbolism of their favorite shared pastime. And because it looked cool. And because it smelled like Jeremy.

"I'm fine." She smiled reassuringly at him. The last year, she had tried so hard to pull off this gruff, nothing-can-hurt-me-now attitude. But, as tough as she was, she still secretly enjoyed the way he always tried to take care of her. The way he thought of her needs before his own. So different from Chad and the way she was used to being treated by a man.

She shook off those bad memories and winked at Jeremy. "And I am holding your jacket hostage. I will let you know the terms of the ransom when I come up with them."

"Are you kidding?" Dylan asked, oblivious to their flirtation. "My mom's always fine. She's totally awesome. She took out that bear armed with only a hiking boot and a roll of toilet paper."

Jeremy laughed. "I agree. Your mom is fairly awesome."

Their laughter was interrupted by the tinkling notes of the theme from *Star Wars* coming from Jeremy's phone.

Maggie shook her head and smiled affectionately. "You are such a nerd."

"I know." Jeremy pulled the latest version of the iPhone from the clip on his belt and studied the readout on the screen. "That's weird—the call is coming from the phone on my desk at the office. I told everyone to take the weekend off."

He touched the little screen and held the phone to his ear. "Hello."

Maggie watched the color drain from Jeremy's face as he listened to the caller.

"Are you sure?" he asked, his shoulders drooping as he rubbed his palm against his forehead. "Okay, I'll be there as soon as I can."

"What's going on?"

Jeremy's face held a stunned expression as he turned to her and clipped the phone back to his belt. "We have to go back to town. Jim Edwards is dead."

"Jim Edwards? The guy from your office?"

"Yeah. Jim is—well, was—one of my programmers. He's helping me create my latest game."

"What happened?"

"I don't know. One of my employees came into work today and found him slumped over his desk. They think he was murdered."

A little over an hour later, Jeremy and Maggie walked into Rogers' Realms to a buzz of activity. Word had spread through the office grapevine, and several of the employees had come in and were milling around, generally getting in the way of the police officers.

Maggie looked around Jeremy's business, her attorney's eye looking for anything unusual or out of place.

The company occupied a large rectangular room. Glassed-in offices framed the perimeter, and four rows of cubicles ran the length of the room, separated by a large center aisle. Jeremy had the biggest corner office, complete with a basketball hoop and a row of big-screen TVs and gaming consoles. A large meeting room with a conference table ran the length of one wall, with a large bank of windows overlooking their small town of Pleasant Valley.

Jeremy headed directly for Jim Edwards's cubicle, and Maggie followed in his wake. The small space looked fairly ordinary, except for Jim's chair lying on its side next to his desk. Much to Maggie's relief, the body had already been removed, and there was no blood in sight, but the area was cordoned off with yellow caution tape.

"You can't be in here, buddy." A young officer held up his hand to stop Jeremy and Maggie.

"I'm Jeremy Rogers. This is my company." He reached for his wallet to present his ID. He motioned to Maggie. "And this is my girlfriend, Maggie Hayes."

Maggie inwardly cringed at the term "girlfriend," but her attention was sidetracked as she saw two little white-haired ladies emerge from Jeremy's office, hot on the heels of a tall police officer. What on earth were they doing here?

Her mouth fell open as she watched the officer turn back to the women and sigh as he ran his hand over his closely shaved head in obvious exasperation. Though Maggie couldn't hear the actual conversation, the women, one wearing a bright red cardigan and the other sporting hot- pink bifocals, were all too familiar to her.

Edna, of the hot-pink glasses, was the senior citizen of their weekly book club, the Pleasant Valley Page Turners. She had been the one who originally tried to set Jeremy up with Sunny, another member of their book club, earlier that summer. Jeremy was the grandson of Edna's best friend Mabel, who now stood behind her, playing Cagney to Edna's Lacey.

Mabel was even shorter than Edna, who stood five foot two in her pink Keds tennis shoes. Mabel's skin carried the tell-tale wrinkles of too much sun. She had the craggy voice and hacking cough of a lifetime smoker, the kind of woman you would see perched on a stool in a Las Vegas casino, a bucket of quarters beside her and a cigarette dangling from her lip as she pulled the slot's handle in between sips of gin and tonic.

Maggie watched Edna pull a small notebook and pen from a huge purple purse and begin to scribble furiously onto the pad. Then, as if by some sonic-Batman-grandma radar, Mabel turned her head, and her face lit up as she caught sight of Jeremy.

She nudged Edna, who looked over, then waved enthusiastically at Maggie. Edna turned back to speak to the officer, who nodded and waved them off as they headed their way.

The young officer handed Jeremy back his ID. "Don't leave. I'm sure someone's gonna wanna talk to you."

"Don't worry. I'm not going anywhere." Jeremy shoved the wallet back into his pocket.

"Don't look now," Maggie said quietly, "but Antique Batman and Robin are headed our way."

Jeremy's look of confusion turned to one of delight as he caught sight of his little grandmother coming toward him. With a few large steps, he covered the distance between them and bent his tall frame to engulf her petite body in his embrace.

He placed a kiss on her leathery cheek and chuckled. "What are you doing here, Gram?"

"Hiya, kiddo. You doing okay?" Mabel's eyes searched his face for signs of stress or shock.

"To tell you the truth, I don't know what I'm doing. I'm shocked. I can't believe this happened. But yeah,

I think I'm okay," he said. "That doesn't answer my question, though. What are *you* doing here?"

"We were driving by your office on the way to our Zumba class at the Y, and we saw all these police cars. We came up to check things out and make sure you were all right." Edna pulled Jeremy's head down to plant a kiss on his cheek. "You all right, kid?"

"I'm fine." Jeremy waved away the women's concern.

"Hey, gals," Maggie said on a rush of air as Edna threw her arms around her in a theatrical embrace. Maggie gave her a quick squeeze, the smell of lavender and vanilla filling the air as she nestled her chin in the cloud of Edna's silver curls. Mabel reached out and squeezed Maggie's hand.

Jeremy seemed to be pleased by the appearance of the two geriatric Nancy Drews, but Maggie's eyes narrowed with suspicion at Edna. "It's amazing how you always seem to be in the middle of whatever excitement is going on."

Edna shrugged and gave her a look of mock innocence. "You know me, honey, if there's a pile of trouble somewhere, I'll find a way to step in it."

Mabel cackled at Edna's joke, then her laugh turned into a phlegmy smoker's cough, and Edna turned to slap her on the back. "You've got to give up those cancer sticks," she said in between slaps.

"Ahh, bite me," wheezed Mabel. "I'm gonna die anyway."

Ignoring the drama of the elderly women, Maggie pulled on Edna's sleeve. "Who is that guy you were talking to? And what did you find out?" Regardless of her knack for finding trouble, Edna was good at ferreting out information and could usually be counted on to know the inside scoop.

"Do they know what happened to Jim?" Jeremy absently rubbed his tiny grandmother's back, used to her frequent coughing fits.

Edna whipped out her notebook, holding it within inches of her nose. "Well, I haven't had a chance to gather too much information, since we just got here and they won't let us too close to the crime scene. I'm sure they're dusting for prints and gathering DNA evidence. The evidence always tells the true story, you know."

"OMG," Maggie said, mimicking one of her son's favorite terms. She tried to control her eyes from rolling into the back of her head as she listened to Edna's *CSI*-esque interpretation of the scene. "What do you *actually* know?"

Edna huffed and lowered her voice. "Well, we know a man was murdered here."

"Oh my gosh. You think? Maybe you should open your own ladies' detective agency."

"I don't get why they think he was murdered," Jeremy said, ignoring Maggie's cheeky comments. "Maybe he had a heart attack or an embolism."

"Can I help you folks?" Their questioning was interrupted by the arrival of the tall, bald-headed officer Edna had been speaking with minutes before.

"This is Officer McCarthy," Edna said, aligning herself with the policeman and resting her hand on his arm. "He and I are old friends. I just call him Mac."

His handsome face took on an amused expression as he looked down at Edna. He covered her hand, completely engulfing her small one in his. "Ms. Allen and I met on another case I worked on earlier this summer."

"He's the one who helped Sunny," Edna explained, alluding to the attack on their mutual friend and fellow book club member several weeks back.

"This is Jeremy, my grandson." Mabel puffed up her chest, not to be outdone by her more dramatic counterpart. "He owns this company."

"Jeremy Rogers," he said, extending his hand.

Officer McCarthy reached out his hand to shake Jeremy's. "I'm Officer McCarthy. I'm the lead officer on this case. You can also call me Mac." Edna held on to his arm like a little monkey clinging to its mother. He turned to Maggie and raised an appreciative eyebrow. "And who might you be?"

Maggie flushed at the obvious flirtation, both annoyed and a little flattered. Before she could respond, Edna stepped in front of her, taking a protective stance.

"She's his lawyer," Edna stated with authority.

Mac's eyes cut back to Jeremy. "Do you think you need a lawyer?"

"No, of course not." Maggie's professional side leapt into action, and she stepped forward, extending her hand. "I'm Maggie Hayes. I *am* a lawyer, but I am here as Jeremy's..." she paused, unable to bring herself to use the *other* term—"friend."

Mac's hand took hers in a grip of strength, his long, lean fingers wrapping around her hand and giving it a firm squeeze.

"My girlfriend," Jeremy clarified, as he watched Mac smile at Maggie. "What do you know about Jim? What happened here?"

Mac stepped back, his face changing to a mask of professionalism as he filled them in on what he knew. "We got a call about two hours ago. A coworker had come in and found Mr. Edwards slumped over his desk. She called 911, but he was apparently already dead."

"Who found him?" Jeremy asked.

Mac pulled a small notebook from his breast pocket and flipped it open. "A Charlotte Foster. I guess finding the body made her a little sick and she keeps going outside to get some fresh air. I haven't had a chance to talk to her yet, but I assume you know her." Edna had also pulled her notebook out again, and Mac sighed as she clicked her pen, ready to record any pertinent information.

Jeremy ignored Edna. "Of course I know her. I know everyone here. Charlotte is one of my programmers. In fact, I think she and Jim have been dating."

Mac scribbled a note down in his pad, and so did Edna. "That's pretty personal information. How well did you know them?"

Jeremy sighed. "Look, it's a small company, and we've all been together for several years. We work late together and occasionally some of us will go for drinks or a meal, especially if we are celebrating a completed project. Do we hang out together? No. But in a small office, you hear what's happening with people, and I knew that Jim and Charlotte were romantically involved."

"And you allow that in the workplace?"

"I don't know. This field is very male dominated. We only have two women who work here and the other one is married, so I haven't really had to worry about it. They're both dedicated employees, and I hadn't noticed it affecting their work, so yeah, I guess I 'allowed' it."

"Did they work together often?"

"Sure. Everybody does. We design and build video game software, and we all work together. The programmers design the game, then the artists go in and build the world. They build every rock, tree, gun, and shoe of the game world. So everyone ends up working with everyone at some point or another to make sure we're producing a cohesive product."

Both Mac and Edna were scribbling notes on their pads. He looked down at her in annoyance. "Quit writing all of this down. I'm the policeman."

Again, Edna's face took on a look of innocence. "Who, me? I'm just jotting down some notes on a new recipe idea I'm thinking of trying."

"Of course you are." Mac turned back to Jeremy.

Before he could open his mouth, Edna asked, "Can you think of anyone who would want to hurt Mr. Edwards?"

Mac looked down at Edna, one eyebrow raised in amazement. "Really?"

Edna shrugged. "Sor-ry." Though she didn't actually look sorry at all.

Mac sighed and returned to his questioning. "So, uh, can you think of anyone who would want to hurt Mr. Edwards or any reason someone would want him dead?"

Jeremy paled at the implication. "No, not at all. Everybody liked Jim. Listen, we're all just a bunch of techie nerds who work here. The most excitement we see is someone high scoring in *Halo* or leveling up in *World of Warcraft*. We all get along fine. I have no idea who could have done this." He looked sadly at Jim's desk.

The whole group turned toward Jim's cubicle in time to see a short, dark-haired man holding a wad of paper towels, reaching to pick up the overturned cup from Jim's desk.

Maggie couldn't believe someone could be naïve enough to be trying to clean up a crime scene. At least it was only coffee that was spilled in the cubicle and not blood.

"Sir, you need to get away from there." Mac's deep voice rose, causing the rest of the room to fall silent.

The young rookie cop who had spoken with Jeremy earlier quickly moved toward the man, but he had already picked up the cup and was blotting at the spilled coffee on the desk.

Mac took three large strides and was beside the man. "Put the cup down and let go of the paper towels. What do you think you're doing? This is a crime scene."

"I know, but that coffee was spilled all over Jim's desk, and he's very careful about keeping his desk neat," the dark-haired man said, still trying to blot at the spilled coffee.

The rest of their merry band had followed Mac to the cubicle. Maggie felt like she was in a group of reporters, all flocking to the next area of interest. Except she didn't find this dweeby guy with the paper towels all that interesting. She wanted to find out more about the actual victim. How was he killed, and why did they think it was murder?

Jeremy introduced the man, who seemed to shrink under Mac's intense gaze. He let go of the paper towels and stood wringing his hands, obviously distressed by all the attention. "This is Leonard Finch. He is one of my artists."

Jeremy lowered his voice and leaned in toward Mac. "He's a little OCD. He likes to keep things in the office neat."

"Jim would hate that coffee spilled all over his desk," Leonard repeated, a dark stain of color rising up along his neck. "It was getting all over his things."

"It's all right, Mr. Finch," Mac said. "We'll make sure the desk is all cleaned up when we're finished here. For now, I need you to step back and let my officers finish up their work, okay?"

"Okay." Leonard took a reluctant step backward. He reached to bring the sodden paper towels with him.

The young officer stepped in front of him and blocked his hand. "We got this," he said.

A loud commotion had the group turning toward the front door of the office as a curvy blonde in her late twenties tried to push past the young cop that had stopped Jeremy earlier.

In an attempt to keep her from passing, the police officer had wrapped one arm around her waist, holding her from entering the room. His face was turning red from the effort and from the fact his arm was pressing against her middle, causing her extremely endowed bosom to push further out of her low-cut, clingy blouse.

Mac looked at Jeremy for confirmation.

He nodded. "It's okay. She works here. That's Charlotte Foster, the one who was dating Jim."

"That's Charlotte?" Mac's eyebrows rose. He had obviously not expected this blonde bombshell to be working in an office primarily filled with engineers and pocket protectors. He waved at the officer to let her through.

She pushed forward, swinging both her purse and her hips as she made her way to them. Long blond hair fell in curly waves around her shoulders. Her makeup was perfect, and her lips shone a glossy shade of red. She wore a black pencil skirt and three-inch high heels, which contributed to the sway in her step. She knew she had the attention of most of the men in the room as she strode forward and threw her arms around Jeremy's neck.

"Oh. My gosh. This is just terrible. I was the one who found him this morning. I came in to catch up on some work, and there he was, slumped over his desk. I thought he was asleep, but he was dead. It was just awful." She looked up at him, a lone tear rolling down her cheek. "How about you? Are you all right, Jeremy?"

Maggie watched as Jeremy awkwardly patted her on the back. She noticed she wasn't the only one watching the exchange. Leonard seemed to be paying close attention as well.

Jeremy untangled Charlotte's arms from around his neck. "I'm fine. I'm more worried about you. How are you holding up?"

"Oh, aren't you just the sweetest thing to be thinking of me." She laid her head back on Jeremy's shoulder, tightening her grip on his neck. "I just feel traumatized. I think I'll have nightmares for weeks. I'm so glad I have a boss like you to turn to. It's going to be hard, but we'll get each other through this."

Maggie raised her eyebrows at Jeremy, who tried again to extract himself from her grasp. Picking jury members had taught her to get a quick read on people, and this gal felt as phony as a three-dollar bill. And her acting skills were atrocious. Maggie just hoped that Jeremy could see through her poor performance and realize she was overacting her part in this drama.

Jeremy pulled Charlotte's arms free of his neck and directed her toward Maggie. "Charlotte, I want you to meet someone. This is the woman I've been telling you about. Maggie Hayes, this is Charlotte Foster, one of my programmers."

"And a friend." Charlotte stuck both her bottom lip and her hand out, the former in an exaggerated pout and the latter in a weak handshake.

One of Maggie's top ten annoyances was a limp handshake, but this woman was quickly working her way up to join the list. Maggie grasped her hand and gave it a firm squeeze, possibly taking a small amount of pleasure in the woman's grimace of pain. "It's nice to meet you, Charlotte. I'm sorry for your loss. This must be very upsetting for you."

Charlotte looked Maggie up and down before tugging her hand back. "So you're the girlfriend. The lawyer." She said the words as if they left a bad taste in her mouth.

Who did this bleach blonde think she was? "Yes, that's me. The lawyer girlfriend." Maggie was surprised at how quickly she owned the term that minutes before she had shunned.

Everything about this woman screamed "meddling, conniving troublemaker" to Maggie. She looked to Jeremy, but he seemed oblivious to the manipulations of his employee.

"Hi. Hi, Charlotte," Leonard said softly from beside Maggie.

She had almost forgotten that he was there. She watched him as he appeared to struggle with getting his next words out.

"How are you doing? Is there anything I can do for you?" Leonard gestured to the hallway behind them. "Can I get you some coffee from the break room or a cup of tea?"

"No thanks, Len. I'm good," Charlotte answered offhandedly as she turned her gaze back to Jeremy.

Leonard turned, his shoulders slumped, and he trudged down the cubicle hallway.

As a lawyer, Maggie was very adept at reading body language and judging people's feelings. Both the adoring look that Charlotte was giving Jeremy and the slouching plod of Len spoke volumes to Maggie's sense of emotions. She glanced over and noticed the way Officer McCarthy was sizing up the players as well. Including her, if the appraising look he gave her now was any indication.

Mac turned his attention back to Jeremy. "Is there anything else you can think of that would help us determine what happened to Mr. Edwards? Anything unusual in his behavior? Any unfamiliar visitors stopping by? Changes in his work habits or hours?"

Jeremy shook his head. "No, nothing. I can't think of any reason someone would want to hurt Jim. He was a good guy."

"Well, if you can think of anything, let me know." Mac fished a business card out of his front pocket and passed it to Jeremy.

"Do you need us to stick around for anything else?" Maggie asked.

"We'll need to get Mr. Rogers's fingerprints for comparison, but after that, you can go." He gestured to the young rookie, who nodded and disappeared down the hall to the break room. "Although we do have one loose end that you might be able to help with."

That loose end was now dragging the rookie police officer back up the hallway. A massive dog covered in thick brown hair pulled at the leash and advanced straight for Maggie. The dog was a cross between a sheep dog and a Newfoundland, with expressive brown eyes and a long snout that was headed directly for Maggie's crotch.

What was it about dogs and their need to sniff people in their private parts? Maggie blocked the dog's nose and patted it on the head. It was wearing a blue collar with the *Star Wars* logo on it. A small plastic toy head of Chewbacca and a tag that read "Chewie" hung from a ring on its collar. "Where did this guy come from?"

Jeremy leaned down and ruffled the big dog's neck. "This is Chewie. He's Jim's dog."

"The victim must have brought him into work with him today," Mac said. "The poor dog was lying on the floor by his side when we got here. We had a hell of a time getting him to let us take the body. It took two officers to get him leashed and locked in the break room."

Aww. Maggie's heart broke for the poor dog.

"The "victim's" name is Jim. And he would sometimes bring Chewie in to work with him. Especially on Saturdays. He loved this dog." Jeremy continued to pat the dog's head.

Chewie sat down on Jeremy's foot, panting loudly. A long line of drool dripped from his mouth onto Jeremy's shoe.

"Do you know if Jim has any family in town or anyone we can call to come get the dog?" Mac asked.

Jeremy looked at Charlotte.

Her face took on a look of horror. "I am not bringing that disgusting beast home with me. I never even let Jim bring it over."

Maggie looked around the room and noticed that suddenly everyone had a job that was requiring their full attention. Several people slipped from the room, and of the remaining few, not one person would make eye contact with Jeremy.

"We can't leave him here," Jeremy said. "What'll happen to him?"

Mac shrugged. "One of my guys will take him down to the animal shelter. Hope someone from the vic—er, Jim's family comes down to claim him."

Chewie cocked his head as if listening to the discussion about his fate. He tipped his head back and let out a mournful howl.

Maggie watched Jeremy, knowing already what he was going to do.

Jeremy looked down at the big dog. "I guess you're coming home with me. Is that all right with you, Chewie?"

The dog barked once, then settled down on the floor next to Jeremy, laying its giant head across his slobber-covered shoe.

Chewie let out a long sigh, and Maggie wasn't sure whom she was falling for more in that moment—the dog or the man who volunteered to take him home.

Mac reached down and patted the dog on the head. "I just wish I knew what this dog saw. He was probably with him when Jim was murdered."

"Poor dog," Jeremy said. "I'll get my fingerprints done, then I'll just take him back to my place. Unless you need anything else."

"Yeah, there is one other thing you can do," Mac said.

Oh geez. The care and feeding of one giant, mangy mutt wasn't enough. Maybe he wanted them to bring a homeless man home too.

The cop smiled at Maggie and gestured to Mabel and Edna. "It's fine if you want to get out of here. Can you just take Sherlock and Holmes with you?"

Being so close to death had Maggie thinking about life and the new life that she had now. The drive back had been somber, and her thoughts had been filled with memories of her past and all the changes that had happened in the past year.

Maggie took in the sight of her two-story home as she and Jeremy pulled up to the curb. She and her ex-husband, now referred to as Chad-the-Cheater, had been so excited when they bought the house. Maggie had just moved up in her law firm, and Chad had found the house in a newer housing development with great parks and good schools for the boys.

"It's all about location, location, location," Chad had told her as he led her around the new house. A smile beamed from his face as he opened doors to show her the walk-in closets and the garden tub in the master bedroom. Chad's smile had been contagious, and she could hear the boys laughing and their sneaker-clad feet running around the tiled floor of the kitchen.

"It's a buyer's market right now," Chad had said, using the lingo of his new profession as a real estate agent. With his charm and good looks, she'd known he would be successful in any type of sales job. She'd loved him so much, and she had loved the house. They bought it, and Drew started kindergarten that year.

Maggie looked at the house now as she stepped out of Jeremy's SUV. Chad was always thinking about curb appeal, and he'd worked tirelessly on landscaping the yard and putting in shrubs and flowerbeds. Maggie could see that a few leaves of the tall aspen trees Chad had planted were just starting to turn gold, and a butterfly alighted in the full purple stalks of the late-summer blooming butterfly bush that grew in front of her porch.

She remembered Chad being so proud of that yard, and she huffed as she thought of the upscale condo he and his Hooters girl, Sapphire, lived in now. With its modern steel and glass décor and manicured lawns, poor Chad had no yard to lovingly care for.

Poor Chad, my foot. He'd been more devoted to that lawn than he ever had been to her or their marriage.

She shook her head to clear the images of Chad-the-Cheater. Why was she thinking of her past when her future was walking her to the front door?

She looked over to Jeremy. He seemed lost in his own reverie of thoughts. Poor guy had just lost one of his favorite employees. A guy he had considered a friend. She reached out and took his hand. "Hey, you okay?"

He blinked and shook his head. Smiling warmly down at her, he squeezed her hand. "Yeah, I'm all right. Just sad, I guess. And confused. Jim was a really nice guy. I don't know why anyone would want to hurt him. I'm really gonna miss the guy."

They stopped in front of Maggie's front door. She slipped her arms around him and pressed her face to his chest. "I'm really sorry."

He tightened his arms around her then slid his hand under her hair to cup her neck as he tilted her face up to his. "Thanks for coming in to the office with me. I really needed you with me today."

Maggie's breath caught as she looked into Jeremy's dark brown eyes. He was so sincere and open with his feelings for her. He said he needed her. Chad wouldn't admit to needing her if his hair was on fire and she was holding a bucket of water.

Even though they had already been dating for about a month now, he was still a perfect gentleman. He opened doors for her and walked her to her front step and always kissed her good night. He knew what a fragile state she was in and seemed content to just be in her presence and take care of her. The few times they had been alone, she knew that he desired her, but he had held back and let her take the lead, knowing she needed to take things slow.

After eighteen years with the same person, she was still getting used to the touch of another man's hand on the small of her back and the feel of different lips on hers.

A warmth spread through her as that other man now leaned down and gently pressed his lips to hers. She tightened her arms around him as he drew her closer and deepened the kiss. Jeremy's hand slid up to grasp a handful of her hair, and he pulled her tighter to him.

His mouth was sweet with the tang of spearmint gum, and Maggie melted into his arms as his lips ravaged hers. He shifted and his mouth moved to trail kisses along her jaw line and down her neck. Her very core tingled as he pressed his head next to hers and breathed, "Oh Maggie," into her ear.

A ripple of tingles ran up her spine as his breath caressed her ear. Then his head dropped to her shoulder and his grip on her waist tightened.

She could feel the mixed emotions running through him as she stood on her front porch and just held on to him. She hadn't known Jim that well but had heard Jeremy tell enough stories about his office to know that he liked the man.

"I should go," he said softly, his voice cracking slightly.

Maggie touched his cheek and held his gaze for an extra heartbeat. "Call me if you need me."

He took her hand from his cheek and gave it a squeeze. "I will," he said, before turning and heading down the driveway toward his car.

The back window of his Toyota 4Runner was down, and Chewie's massive head hung out the open space. The dog gave a quick bark, which Maggie took as a goodbye. Although it easily could have meant "you have a nice lawn," or "please don't leave," or "hey, look, a squirrel."

Maggie pulled her keys from her purse, unlocked the front door, and let out a deep sigh as she stepped into her front room.

Before she could finish the sigh, her eyes narrowed, and she looked skeptically around the room. Something felt off.

Nothing seemed outwardly amiss. The burgundy leather sofa was neat; the striped throw pillows lay against one padded armrest. The coffee table held a book filled with recipes she would never make, which lay artfully arranged next to a Pottery Barn candelabra holding a thick cream-colored candle. The sounds of the latest video game could be heard faintly drifting in from the living room, hidden on the other side of the kitchen.

Everything seemed tidy, as usual, but Maggie detected a new scent in the air. Actually, an old scent, a very familiar old scent of Polo and Irish Spring.

It couldn't be! A different kind of sigh escaped her as she caught sight of the one thing out of place in the room. A large, black duffle bag sat in the kitchen doorway, a Miami Dolphins bumper sticker splayed across one seam and the zipper bulging against a light blue t-shirt trying to escape.

Chad-the-Cheater was back.

Maggie's teeth clenched as she set her purse down on the sofa. Before she could speak, the click of tiny toenails and a pair of too-large feet could be heard as Dylan and her Scottish terrier, Barney, came bursting through the kitchen door.

"Mom! Guess what?" Dylan cried as he launched himself at her and threw his arms around her neck. "Dad's here!"

While happy to get a rare hug from her youngest son, she was annoyed that Chad's return had prompted it. Maggie took advantage of the moment to squeeze Dylan against her, as she murmured, "So I see."

Dylan radiated with excitement. "Isn't that great, Mom? Dad is back! He had a *big* fight with Sapphire, and she broke up with him, and so now he's back and he wants to stay here. I told him it would be fine with us. It is fine with us, right, Mom? Mom?"

Her son's frantic flow of words seemed to suck the breath from Maggie's lungs, and her heart beat faster as the pace of his voice accelerated. "Great" was not exactly the word she had in mind when she thought about Chad.

Stunned, she sank to the couch, so mindless that she landed on her Coach bag, and her left cheek was probably smashing a lip gloss and a pack of gum. "Did you say 'stay here'?" she croaked.

"Just for a few days, a week at the most," a deep male voice said from the kitchen doorway. Maggie whipped her head around to see her ex-husband leaning against the door-jamb, a sheepish grin on his face. "Hi, Maggie-May."

Maggie's mouth opened and closed, but no words seemed to form as she took in the sight of her ex-husband. She hadn't seen him in months and she hated to admit he looked pretty good. The hair plugs Sapphire had insisted on had grown in and seemed more natural as they blended with his dark hair. His teeth looked whiter against his tan skin, and he wore shorts, flip-flops, and a clichéd Ed Hardy shirt that screamed, "Recently divorced and trying to recapture my youth."

He had always been good-looking, but he'd dropped ten or fifteen pounds and seemed to be in better shape than he had the last five years of their marriage. *I guess having a younger girlfriend is good incentive for working out*, Maggie thought. *Maybe I should think about getting one.*

"What are you doing here?" she finally managed to ask. "And don't call me Maggie-May."

Chad nodded to Dylan. "Hey, kid, why don't you go up to your room for a bit? Give your mom and me a chance to talk."

"Okay, Dad." Like a golden retriever, happy to please its master, Dylan headed for the stairs. Stopping at the first step, he turned back to face his father. "You won't leave while I'm up there, will you?"

A fist of pain clutched at Maggie's heart as she heard the subtle desperation in her son's voice. As angry as the boys were at the man who had cheated on their mother, they both still missed their dad. At fourteen, Dylan was often pulled between those feelings of anger and the desire to have his father around. Maggie knew that Dylan harbored the secret hope that his parents would get back together and things would go back to the way they were.

Maggie feared that Dylan's enthusiasm at his Dad's return might be the result of that hope.

Chad waved away Dylan's concern. "No way, I'll still be here." He flashed Maggie a used-car salesman grin. "Unless your mom kicks me out…"

Seriously? Was he flirting with her? The pain turned to "pissed," and Maggie propelled herself off the sofa. "Dylan, go on up to your room and let me talk to your dad. He won't leave without saying goodbye."

She pointed at Chad. "You, in the kitchen. Now."

Chad ducked his head sheepishly, and stepped back into the kitchen. "Hey, no need to get hostile."

Maggie followed him into the room, the little dog close on her heels. Chad pointed to the tall stool that sat against the kitchen's center island. "Let me get you something to drink, and we can just talk." He used his soothing voice as he pulled two glasses from the cabinet above the sink and filled them with ice.

He opened the refrigerator, grabbed a Diet Coke, and scanned the remaining contents of the fridge. "Don't we have any beer?"

Maggie shook her head incredulously. "No, *I* don't have any beer. I have teenage boys, and they don't need the temptation of beer in the house. Besides, *I* don't even like beer! And in case you've forgotten, this is *my* house and *my* refrigerator and I can keep whatever I damn well please in it." She blew her dark bangs out of her eyes.

"Geez, you don't have to get all snippy about it," Chad said. "I'll just have a Diet Coke too." He popped the tops of the two cans and poured the soda into the two glasses, then handed one to Maggie.

She took a deep breath then a long sip of the sweet liquid. How many fights had they had where Chad's voice had calmed while hers became more anxious? She took one more sip, using the drink as an excuse to calm her nerves. "What are you doing here, Chad?"

"Well, you see, um..." Chad looked at everything in the room except for her. "Sapphire and I sort of got in this fight, and she sort of kicked me out."

"Then why don't you 'sort of' stay in a hotel? What are you doing *here*?"

"Well, you see..."

"No, I don't see. What is going on? Quit stalling and spit it out!" Maggie said, using a cross between her "defense attorney" and "mom" voices.

"She spent all my money, and I can't afford to stay in a hotel," Chad said, all in one breath. "There. Are you happy?"

Mmmm, just a little, she thought. But what she said was: "No, I'm not happy. I am annoyed that you are here, disrupting our lives."

"Hey, this used to be my life too."

"*Used* to be is right," Maggie said, her voice rising again. Before it could reach skyscraper level, the front door banged open and Maggie groaned as she heard her oldest son, Drew, calling for her.

"Mom! Hey, Mom! My acceptance letter from Colorado State University was in the mailbox when we got home." He flew into the kitchen, a look of pure joy on his face.

His look quickly turned to one of suspicion as he saw his father leaning against the counter. "What are you doing here?"

"Hi, Drew." Chad pushed off from the counter and extended his hand to his son.

Drew kept his hands loosely at his sides. "I said, what are you—"

The sound of Dylan's excited voice and his feet clambering down the stairs broke into Drew's sentence. "Drew! Drew! You won't believe it!" The boy tumbled into the kitchen, almost colliding with his older brother. "Drew! Dad's here. Did you see? Dad's here! And he's gonna stay with us!"

Drew turned to Maggie, an incredulous look on his face. "He's what?"

"Okay, hold on, bud," Maggie said to Dylan. "No one said he's staying."

"Oh, but c'mon, Mom, you gotta let him stay. He doesn't have anywhere else to go," Dylan whined.

"The boy has a point," Chad said, a satisfied grin on his face. He leaned back against the counter, content to watch his son plead his case for him.

Drew looked questioningly at his mother, silent understanding flowing between them—of the struggle of making Dylan this happy and kicking Chad-the-Cheater out on his keester.

"C'mon, Mom, it's just for a few days." Dylan moved to stand next to his father. He'd grown several inches over the summer and, at five foot ten, now stood almost as tall as Chad. "And I'll even help clean up the house more. I can unload the dishwasher tonight. And Dad will help too, won't you, Dad?"

He looked at his father, who smiled and put his arm around his son's shoulder. "Of course I will. I'm pretty good with running the vacuum. C'mon, Maggie, what d'ya say?"

Maggie felt her resolve melting as Dylan's eyes pleaded with her. Having Chad here seemed to make her son so happy, and she would do just about anything to keep that smile on his face. Even if it meant putting up with her ex. "Well, if it's only for a few days…"

"A week, tops," Chad assured her.

"Mom!" Drew said, giving his mother his best, "what-the-hell-are-you-thinking?" glare.

Maggie shrugged and nodded at Dylan. "It's only for a few days."

Drew's eyebrows rose.

"A week, tops," Chad said again, clapping Dylan on the shoulder. "I'll sleep in the extra bunk bed in Dylan's room. It'll be like a camp-out."

He looked toward Maggie. "You won't even know I'm here. I'll be gone before you know it. I've got a couple things lined up, I just need to get my feet back under me."

Hmmm, Maggie thought. *Where have I heard that before?*

"So someone was really murdered at Jeremy's office?" Sunny asked.

"Yep." Maggie set Diet Cokes in front of Sunny and Cassie, her best friends since college. "I can't believe I haven't had a chance to talk to you guys yet."

The last few days had flown by in a whirlwind of activity. Suddenly, Wednesday night was here, and Maggie was hosting their weekly book club meeting at her house.

Luckily, she had given the bakery down the block from her office building the schedule of her meeting nights and they had two of her customary scrumptious desserts boxed and waiting for her when she ran in at six o'clock that evening.

"His name was Jim, and he was poisoned. Jeremy called last night and told me that the cause of death was some kind of poison in his coffee cup." Maggie sliced into one of the desserts and placed a thick piece of chocolate mousse cake onto a plate before passing it to Sunny.

Maggie filled them in on all the details while also filling the other three plates: another large piece of chocolate cake for Piper, who at eighteen, could still eat whatever she wanted; a small piece of the Boston cream pie for Cassie, who was always watching her weight; and a small slice of each on a plate for Edna, who claimed she liked to have her cake and eat it too.

"And Edna was there?" Cassie asked. She wore her standard "mom" outfit of jeans and a t-shirt. Her blond hair was pulled into a clip, a few loose tendrils of curls escaping the fastener. Her shining eyes and upturned nose gave her a cute pixie-face appeal, and the few extra pounds she was always complaining about actually looked good on her petite frame. Her door and her arms were always open, and she was the first to give out hugs, usually followed by cookies.

She pulled the plate toward her and swiped a finger through the middle section of pudding. Bringing a large dollop of yellow cream into her mouth, Cassie closed her eyes and groaned in pleasure at the delicious vanilla flavor.

"Of course she was," Maggie said, then turned to Sunny. "But where is she now? Why didn't she come with you?" Sunny lived a few doors down from Edna, and they usually carpooled to book club each week.

"She had an exercise class downtown, so Piper is picking her up after her class and bringing her over," Sunny explained.

The front door opened, and the sound of Edna's voice carried into the kitchen as she doled out her characteristic advice to anyone who would listen.

"Speak of the she-devil now," Maggie said with a smirk, then her jaw dropped as Edna walked into the kitchen. "Oh. My. Gosh! What are you wearing?"

Edna had on a tight pink sweatsuit over a lime-green tank top. A pink and white braided head-band circled her silvery curls.

"What?" Edna asked, turning in a circle. "This is my new exercise outfit."

The women exploded into laughter as Edna turned, displaying the word "Juicy" spelled out in hot-pink letters across her backside.

"Edna," Sunny gasped between fits of giggles. "Where on earth did you buy some Juicy Couture?"

"Isn't it cute? I got this down at the Goodwill a couple of weeks ago. Mabel and I signed up for a Zumba class, and I needed a new sweatsuit. I loved the color, and got it marked down from $7.99 to $2.49 with my senior discount. I like it. It kind of makes me feel sassy." Edna winked as she gave her behind a little wiggle.

Which only set the women off on another round of hysterical laughter.

"You *are* sassy." Sunny wiped the tears from her eyes with the corner of her napkin. The antics of her neighbor never failed to amuse her. True to her name, Sunny's bright personality worked perfectly with her job as an elementary school teacher. She was of average build and height, and her friends envied her shoulder-length, naturally curly blond hair. Her easy laugh and positive spirit also contributed to her *Sunny* disposition.

"Well, I like her new sweatpants." Piper smiled at Edna. "I think they make you look hot."

"Ha! See there. Piper thinks I look hot." Edna gave a satisfied huff. "So the rest of you can just shut up and eat your cake."

Piper laughed, dropped her bulging back pack on the floor, and sank into a chair at the kitchen table. "Speaking of cake, can someone pass me a plate? I'm starving."

Cassie picked up the plate with the large piece of chocolate cake covering it. She passed it across to the table but halted midway as a man wearing a white t-shirt and pajama pants walked into the kitchen.

Both her mouth and the plate fell, and the only sound in the room was tiny toenails on the kitchen floor as Barney raced into the room and frantically began eating the fallen cake.

Cassie could only gape at the man, who casually cut himself a piece of the dessert.

"Hello, ladies," Chad said, a slow grin crossing his face, as if he were just daring them to question his arrival.

Edna, never afraid of a dare, was the first to speak. "What in the Sam hell are *you* doing here?"

"Just getting a piece of cake. I always did love book club night." He picked up a fork and stuck a large bite of chocolate cake in his mouth. "The dog really shouldn't eat all that chocolate," he said around the bite of cake as he gestured to the dog with his fork.

"Then neither should you," Edna retorted. "I've heard chocolate is bad for dogs."

Maggie shooed the dog away as she scooped up the remains of the cake with a napkin. Cleaning up the mess gave her something to focus on so she didn't have to look into the eyes of the women who knew her so well.

"Maggie?" Sunny asked, not able to phrase anything more than the one word.

Maggie tossed the mess into the trash while giving Chad a look of exasperation. "Really?"

"What? I just wanted some cake." Chad shrugged, doing his best to look innocent.

"What are you doing here?" Edna repeated. "And why are you in your pajamas at six thirty at night? Don't you have a job?"

Chad's grin faded. "Look, I'm just between jobs right now—"

"Chad, just take the cake and go upstairs," Maggie said before he could make things worse.

"Fine." He took his plate and left the kitchen, Barney following close at his heels, the dog's only allegiance to whomever currently had cake.

The women of the Pleasant Valley Page Turners stared expectantly at Maggie as she washed her hands and began wiping crumbs off the kitchen counter.

"Well?" Edna said, propping her hands on her hips. "Are you gonna tell us what that no-job, cake-eating, pajama-wearing cheat of an ex-husband is doing here? Or are you just gonna ignore us and wipe down the counter and act like that little scene didn't just happen?"

"I'll choose to wipe down the counters and act like nothing happened."

"Maggie!" Cassie and Sunny cried in unison.

Maggie threw the dishcloth in the sink and sighed. "Sapphire spent all his money and kicked him out. When he showed up here, Dylan was so excited to see his dad that I agreed to let him stay here for a *few* days. End of story." She picked up a fork, stabbed a large bite of chocolate cake, and stuffed it into her mouth.

"That is sooo not the end of the story," Sunny said. "Why isn't he working? Why did he come here? Why didn't he stay with a friend?"

As Sunny shot rapid-fire questions at Maggie, Cassie walked around the counter to enfold their friend into a hug.

"I don't know how it happened." Maggie's voice was muffled as she spoke into Cassie's shoulder. "He was just here, and Dylan was so happy, and I was worried about Jeremy and it didn't seem like that big of a deal. And it's only for a few days."

"Hmmph!" Edna still had not removed her hands from her hips. "How is it you can be so tough in the courtroom, but you let this guy walk all over you?"

Maggie shook her head. "I don't know. I was married to the guy, so he knows how to push my buttons and get me to cave. In this case, that button was Dylan. Don't worry, I'm making sure he's looking for another place to stay."

The women looked at Maggie, not sure how to respond. Their silence was broken by the strains of Lady Gaga's "Poker Face" coming from somewhere in Edna's vicinity.

Edna reached into her tank top and pulled a cell phone from her bra. Pushing a button, she snapped into the phone, "What do you want, you old bat?"

Whatever the "old bat" had to say must not have been good, because Edna's face fell and she told the caller, "I'm with Maggie now. We'll be right there," before ending the call and shoving the phone back into her bra.

"What's going on?" Maggie asked.

"Grab your purse, we're going to the police station," Edna said. "Jeremy's been arrested. C'mon, I'll drive."

"He's not under arrest." Officer McCarthy shook his head at the group of women crammed into the front office of the Pleasant Valley Police Station. "Why did you *all* think you needed to show up? There hasn't been this many people in here since the Clapshaw twins accidentally drove their dad's truck into the side of the Tastee-Freez."

Maggie looked around the crowded reception area. The five members of the Page Turners book club had filled the small space, and Jeremy's tiny grandmother had walked in a few minutes after they arrived with enough stuff to take the space of two people.

Mabel carried her handbag on her wrist and a purple tote the size of Texas over her shoulder. To Maggie's surprise, she noticed a red and white bucket of fried chicken tucked under the older woman's arm.

"I wasn't sure how long we'd have to wait." Mabel gestured to the bag. "I brought a few paperbacks and my laptop in case I need to update my status on Facebook. I hope they have Wi-Fi here."

Edna nodded at her friend. "That was good thinking, Mabel. We may need to Google a good bail bondsman too."

Mac rolled his eyes. "I told you. He is *not* under arrest."

"If he's not under arrest, why'd you stick him in the police car and then throw him in the pokie?" Edna pointed a bony, wrinkled finger at the officer.

Mac sighed. "First off, Ms. Allen, he is not in the 'pokie.' And second of all, I put him in the police car because that is what this fine city gives me to drive. Did you want me to load him on the back of my motorcycle?"

"You have a motorcycle?" Cassie asked. She wiggled her eyebrows at Sunny and Maggie.

Sunny ignored her friend and turned to Officer McCarthy. "Then why is he here?"

"Hi, Sunny." Mac's face softened. He had been the officer on the scene earlier that summer when she had been assaulted, and it was obvious from his smile that he had a soft spot for Sunny. "How you doin'? Do you have to bring Edna along every time I see you?"

Sunny grinned. "We're kind of a package deal, I think. What can you tell us about Jeremy?"

"Like I said, he's not under arrest. We just brought him down for questioning."

"Has he asked for his lawyer yet?" Maggie's voice held an edge of ice. She was not here to smile and play nice with the policeman. No matter how cute he was. She was here to find out about Jeremy.

She wore high-heeled boots and stood well above the other shorter women. Mac looked up and his gaze met Maggie's. His voice held a touch of challenge. "Does he need one?"

Maggie had never been intimidated by men in power. "You tell me."

Mac stared at her for an extra beat, then held his hands up in surrender. "Look, ladies, there's no reason to get upset and start calling in the lawyers. In case I need to state the obvious, someone was *murdered* at *his* company. Of course we're going to want to ask him some questions." He waved a hand at the group. "And furthermore, we may have to talk to him several times, and I don't need the Nancy Drew Detective Agency Book Club filling up my police station every time we ask him to come down."

"So, is he free to go?" Maggie asked, ignoring the sarcasm aimed at the Page Turners.

"We're going over a few things with him. It may be a while."

The women looked at each other, and Maggie shrugged. "I guess I'll wait for him. There's no need for everybody to stick around."

Sunny put her hand on Maggie's shoulder. "We can wait with you. We could just have our book club discussion here."

Piper nodded. "We can totally stay with you."

Maggie looked around the entry room of the small police station. A scarred wooden bench sat along one wall, possibly long enough to fit three people on. If they were supermodels or hadn't eaten much in the last few weeks. "It's all right. Why don't you just take everyone home? I have some emails to catch up on. I can use my phone and do a little work while I'm here."

"That's okay with me," Cassie said. "I still have to make cupcakes for Tiffany's class tonight, and I hate to admit it, but I didn't finish reading the book this week anyway."

"What else is new?" Sunny said.

Edna planted her bony bottom on the bench seat. "Well, I already had cake tonight, and that's the main reason I come to book club, so I can stay and wait with her. I have some ideas about this murder. Maybe I can find a detective to run some theories by." She looked hopefully at Mac, who just shook his head.

Mabel plopped down next to Edna. She opened the bucket of chicken and pulled out a leg. "Yeah, I can stay too. There's nothing but reruns on the tube tonight, anyway. Maybe we'll get lucky and they'll bring in an *actual* criminal. Then we can see some real police work in action."

The dig in Mabel's statement was obviously not lost on Officer McCarthy. "Nobody needs to wait. It could be hours before he's done. One of the officers will give him a ride home. And I don't need you filling up my reception area. It's bad enough to have criminals in here; we don't need a book club meeting going on too."

He pointed at Edna. "And get this one out of here. Knowing her, she's probably got a concealed weapon somewhere in that handbag she's carrying. And what old lady goes around wearing sweatpants with JUICY printed on her behind?"

Edna looked around the room, clutching her large purse a little closer to her chest and not making eye contact with Mac.

"Nobody has to wait with me." Maggie motioned to the group. "Really. You all go on home. I'll call you tomorrow."

"All right. We'll clear out." Sunny leaned in to give Maggie a quick hug. "Give me your keys. We'll pick up your car and leave it here in the parking lot so you can take Jeremy home."

Maggie dug her key ring from her purse. She had forgotten that they had all ridden over with Sunny. Edna had offered to drive, but that would have been a ride they all would've remembered. "Thanks, Sunny."

"Of course. Call me if you need me." She gave Maggie's shoulder a quick squeeze then gestured to the women filling up the reception area of the small-town police station. "Let's go, ladies. The Sunny Bus is leaving, and you all have two minutes to get on it."

Edna and Mabel grumbled as they pushed up from the bench. Mabel held the bucket out to Maggie. "Want me to leave the chicken?"

"No, thanks." Maggie watched them head for the door as she sank onto the bench Edna and Mabel had vacated.

Edna turned and waved a hand at Officer Mac. "Stay tough out there, Mac. We'll talk soon."

Mac waved and shook his head. Maggie heard him mumble, "I can't wait."

Two hours, thirty-five emails and three levels of *Candy Crush* later, Maggie was still waiting. She stretched her legs in front of her and yawned, wishing now that Mabel had left the bucket of fried chicken.

Sunny had dropped her keys and a bottle of Diet Coke by over an hour ago. The now empty pop bottle on the floor by Maggie's feet prompted her full bladder to kick in with a *gotta go right now* message.

Before she had a chance to ask the bored-looking desk officer where she would find a ladies' room, the front door opened and a husky female officer escorted a woman in handcuffs into the police station and dumped her on the bench next to Maggie.

The woman was attractive, yet had that "too many nights sitting in a bar" look about her. She turned to Maggie and flashed her a friendly smile. "I love your boots." Her voice held a slight Southern drawl, but the compliment seemed sincere.

Maggie studied the woman. Her long dark-blond hair curled around her face, with two inches of roots signaling that she hadn't been to the salon in several months. The woman was slim and appeared to be in her late forties. She had a small waist and ample cleavage spilled out of the V-neck of her black t-shirt, a *Sons of Anarchy* emblem displayed across her chest. She wore red spike heels with black low-rise jeans, and Maggie spotted a butterfly tattoo across her back as the woman bent forward to drop her huge hobo bag on the floor.

She slumped back against the seat, the smell of cigarettes and perfume wafting off of her tanned skin. "Hey, honey. I'm Lori. Lori Waddle. I'd shake your hand, but..." She lifted her shackled wrists toward Maggie.

"Maggie."

Lori looked her over. "What'd they get you for? Harassing the PTA or stealing Girl Scout cookies?"

Maggie laughed. "I'm just waiting for a friend."

"That's all I was doing too. Just waiting for a friend. And Miss Piggy in a policeman's uniform came over and arrested me." She raised her voice and aimed her comment at the stout female police officer. "Hey, you should ask them for a uniform that's in your *actual* size. And that color is not flattering."

"Pipe down." The policewoman adjusted the brown uniform top, pulling together the gaping edges straining to hold the buttons in place. Her gold name-tag read "Officer Crane." "We can't all be fashion models like you."

The woman shrugged. "You don't have to be mean about it. I'm just saying that uniform isn't the most slimming. And a little mascara and lip gloss wouldn't hurt you."

Maggie noted the thick layers of mascara and eye shadow that her bench-mate wore, and wasn't sure she should be dispensing make-up advice. Something about the woman amused Maggie, though, and watching their interaction gave her something to do besides worry about what was taking Jeremy so long and how much she needed to use the bathroom.

Lori turned to Maggie again. "Really, I wasn't even doing anything. I was over at the Travel Inn, out on the highway there, the one with the nice lounge in it. I was just minding my own business. Wasn't doing anything wrong."

"Last time I checked, prostitution was illegal in Colorado," Officer Crane commented from the counter, her head bent over a clipboard of papers she was filling in.

"Prostitution? Who are you calling a prostitute?" Lori threw back her shoulders with exaggerated indignation and turned to Maggie. "Do I look like a hooker to you?"

Maggie kept wisely silent.

"I just met this nice man, and we got to talking. It's a free country for men and women to talk to each other."

The policewoman didn't even look up as she bantered back: "And you needed to finish that conversation in your hotel room? And then charge him a hundred dollars for your talk? You must have had some pretty wise pearls of wisdom to share."

Lori winked at Maggie. "Oh, I did. I am a pretty great conversationalist. And I didn't charge him for anything. That was just a gift. Between friends."

"Well, you might see your 'friend' later. In court. And you might see your new friend there too." Officer Crane pointed her ball point pen at Maggie. "You're telling your troubles to a lawyer."

Lori swiveled back to Maggie and raised an eyebrow. "You really a lawyer?"

Maggie shrugged. "Guilty as charged." She loved a good lawyer pun.

"Do you ever take any of those Sonny Bono cases?"

Maggie looked at her questioningly.

"You know. When the people don't have enough money to pay."

Ah. The light bulb clicked on. "You mean pro bono."

"Yeah. Isn't that what I said?" Lori leaned in toward Maggie. "Do you ever take on those cases?"

The door to the back room opened, saving Maggie from answering. A bedraggled Jeremy stepped through, and Maggie was surprised at the emotion she felt for him. She wanted to wrap her arms around him and tell him everything would be all right. She only hoped that was true.

She stood and crossed the room. Before she could speak, he folded her into his arms and held her tight against him. She felt him inhale and he held her just a beat too long.

Maggie pulled back and looked up into his weary brown eyes. "You okay?"

"I will be. Thanks for coming to get me." He looked around the reception area. "The officer said the whole book club was here, including my granny."

Maggie chuckled. "They were here. I sent them home."

Jeremy ran a hand through his already mussed hair. "Home sounds good. Let's get out of here."

"Good idea." Maggie crossed back to the bench, dug a business card from her purse, and passed it to her new friend. "Here's my card. You can give my office a call. I'll see if I can help."

"Hey, thanks." Lori lifted her cuffed hands and took the card, holding it tightly between her fingers. She winked up at Maggie. "By the way, your friend's a hottie."

Maggie looked at Jeremy. He *was* kind of a hottie. But right now, he was in *hot* water. Maggie hoped she had the strength to get him out.

The drive to Jeremy's house seemed to take two hours instead of ten minutes. Jeremy was unusually quiet. Maggie was used to his constant chatter about some new idea he was working on. But tonight, he had no ideas.

Jeremy's somber mood was broken for a moment as he opened the front door and Chewie came lumbering into the room, his huge hind end shaking with the excitement of Jeremy being home.

They made their way into the kitchen, and Jeremy slumped into one of the tall chairs that sat up against the center island. The big dog lay at his feet, resting his furry head on Jeremy's foot.

Fairly at home in his kitchen, Maggie poured them each a glass of wine, then walked around the counter and placed one in front of Jeremy.

"Thanks." He took a sip, then pulled Maggie to him, encircling her with his arms and tugging her into his lap. He leaned his head against hers. "Well, that sucked."

Maggie laughed. "Yeah, I bet. Do they know anything? Could you tell if they had any leads?" What she really wanted to know was why they questioned him for so long and what they thought they had against him.

"They didn't tell me anything. They just asked me to go over the same stuff. They asked me to tell them about everyone in the office. They asked about Jim and Charlotte and their relationship and if anybody else was having a relationship in the office. And if I had any relationships in the office."

Maggie looked at Jeremy but wisely kept her mouth closed.

"I didn't. I'm the boss. That's a line I don't cross," he assured her. "Besides, we only have two women that even work there. One is happily married, and the other is Charlotte. Unfortunately, I don't think Jim is the first office romance that she's had, but I usually stay out of that stuff. I have enough other things to worry about than who is hooking up with whom."

Maggie thought back to the eye-popping cleavage that Charlotte was sporting and could easily imagine that she enjoyed the attention of the other men in the office. Granted, the woman did have a nice set of ta-tas, but were they worth killing someone over? "What else did they ask you about?"

"They spent a lot of time talking about our new game and our competitor, SkyVision. Someone at the company must have told the police that we had a pretty strong rivalry with SkyVision, because the cops spent, like, an hour just asking me about their company and how our new game is competing with theirs."

Maggie took a sip of her wine and leaned against Jeremy. "And…how does it compete?"

"It doesn't." Jeremy shook his head. "Nobody's does. This new game that we're working on is like nothing the gaming world has ever seen before. The programming of the artificial intelligence is so advanced, it's going to blow everything else out of the water."

"So, you could potentially make a lot of money with this gaming thing?"

"'A lot of money' is an understatement. It has the potential to outsell anything we've designed before. This new game is worth millions of dollars in revenue."

Maggie knew that Jeremy was well off and that his company was successful. He lived a fairly modest lifestyle, but in the several weeks that she had been dating him, she noticed a few things that hinted at his wealth.

He owned a nice house in an upscale neighborhood, but his home had a few additions. The entry way and kitchen floors were Italian marble, and Maggie knew the thick, luxurious rugs covering the floors had to be quite expensive. The kitchen itself held top-of-the-line appliances, including a well-stocked wine cellar hidden behind the pantry.

The floors of the bathroom were heated, and the bathtub in the master bath was big enough to hold four people. Jeremy enjoyed recreational activities and had an in-ground pool and hot tub installed in the backyard, as well as a fenced-in basketball court. A large room in his basement was converted into a theater room, with several comfy recliners, a ginormous big-screen TV, and a state-of-the-art sound system.

The last game that Jeremy's company had produced had netted him a substantial income. If this new game was worth even more money, then that was definitely a motive for murder.

"Who else knew about this new game and its capabilities?" she asked.

"Not that many people. We were trying to keep it pretty hush-hush. But the gaming world is actually pretty small, and we're a tight-knit group. I'm sure word of this could easily have leaked out."

"Could Jim be the one who leaked it?"

"Sure. Anybody could have leaked it." Jeremy sighed and ran his hand through his hair. "My whole company knew about it. We talk about it in staff meetings, and we have been working up promotional material on it for months. Producing a game like this is so complicated that a lot of people have a hand in it."

"How well do you—did you—trust Jim?"

Jeremy grinned at her. "You're starting to sound like a lawyer."

"That's because I *am* a lawyer. Answer the question."

"All right. Geez." He looked into his glass as he swirled the wine inside, as if he were searching for answers in the amber liquid. "I thought I could trust him. But I think I can trust everyone that I work with. They all sign an extensive packet of waivers and contracts defining their rights, and everything they design under our company belongs to us. They also each sign confidentiality clauses, so they are prohibited from talking about or sharing any of our designs."

Now he was talking her language. Clauses and contracts and waivers—she knew about these things. Most of the things Jeremy told her about his company were in a language she didn't even comprehend. "Have you heard anybody talking about leaking information or being unhappy at work?"

"No. I haven't heard anything. I feel like we're one big happy family."

His cell phone vibrated on the counter, and Maggie read Charlotte's name on the display. *And there's one of the family calling now.* From her vantage point, she could read the text message: *Just thinking about you. Hope you are okay.*

Maggie watched Jeremy pick up the phone and return the text: *thanks. I'm fine.* He didn't seem to try to hide the message or be uncomfortable with the text. "Does she text you after hours a lot?"

"Sure. We all do. I work with so many people in their twenties, that's the only way they know how to communicate. You can't get them on the phone, but send a text and they reply within seconds."

Maggie knew this to be true with her own kids. But still, something about Charlotte's text felt a little too familiar for a message to her boss. The phone buzzed again, and Maggie could see the new message pop up on the screen: *I've been worried about you. Do you want me to pop over and keep you company for a while?*

Pop over? What was she talking about? Every one of Maggie's instincts went on high alert. "Does she come over here often?"

"I wouldn't say often, but she's been here. I have everybody over every few months. They like to use the pool in the summer or hang out and watch movies. We can be relaxed and talk about the games we're working on or mess around playing them. Some of those guys are their most creative when they're just sitting around with a controller in their hands."

She hated herself for asking, but couldn't help it: "But Charlotte—does she come over here? By herself?"

Jeremy gave her a questioning look. "No, she usually shows up with a bunch of the guys. They like to get her to bring home-cooked food for them." A crooked grin crossed his face as he obviously figured out why she was asking. "Are you jealous?"

Maggie huffed in indignation. "Me? Jealous? Of her? No, of course not." But it had been a waitress at a restaurant that had shown her husband enough attention to make him leave, so nothing would surprise her anymore. "She's just making herself very available to you. It seems like she should be grieving her current boyfriend, not trying to hook a new one."

"Come on. That's ridiculous. She would never be interested in me. I'm much older than she is and way too nerdy."

Maggie shook her head. Jeremy must have been really geeky in high school, because he always seemed to underestimate how attractive he was. Sure, he carried a little scent of nerd on him, but in a good way. She liked that he was cute and not conceited about his good looks. "You are not too old for her and some girls really go for those handsome, nerdy types."

"You think I'm handsome?" Jeremy's face broke into a grin, and he playfully pulled her closer to him. "I still can't believe I got you to fall for me."

"Who says I have?" But she knew that she had. And she was falling more for him every day that she spent with him. That was why she hated this jealous, green-eyed monster that was creeping out from under her perfectly made bed.

"Don't worry. There is absolutely nothing between Charlotte and me. Never has been and never will be." Jeremy typed in a message and held the screen up for Maggie to see. *No thanks. Maggie is here and she is all the company I need. See you at work on Monday.*

"Does that make you feel better?

"I felt fine before." But she did feel better. A little. "You don't have to prove anything to me."

"I know. But I want to." He slid his hand up to touch her cheek. "I know you've been hurt before. And I don't want to ever be the guy who hurts you. I really care about you, Maggie, and I want this to work."

Maggie raised her hand and rested it on his. She looked into his brown eyes, and saw such sincerity in them, she fell a little harder. "I know. I do too." And she did want it to work. She hated the feeling of never being able to trust a man and of her constant suspicions. She needed to accept that women would be interested in Jeremy and trust that he would be faithful to her.

But that was her problem. Trust. She tried to push her suspicions aside and believe in Jeremy. He was like a golden retriever, so cuddly and always trying to please her. But cute puppies could still chew up your favorite shoes and poop on your floor.

Jeremy took her hand. "Hey, don't worry. Everything is going to be fine. You'll see." He pulled her closer and brushed her cheek with a gentle kiss. His lips trailed light kisses along her cheek until his mouth met hers and he lingered there, each tender kiss an invitation to more.

Maggie leaned into him, giving herself to the rush of heat that grew in her chest and the feel of his lips on hers. She kissed him back, taking the soft kisses to a deeper level. She tasted the wine he had been drinking and breathed in the masculine scent of the aftershave that still clung to his skin.

She needed this. She needed to lose herself in his touch. To forget the horrors of the past few days. Of murder scenes and police stations and doubts over busty, flirtatious blondes. To just be with Jeremy. To feel his hands on the small of her back, pulling her tighter against him.

She loved the way he kissed her. He had this way of being tentative and shy, and yet she could feel his hunger and passion bubbling just below the surface. As if they were in high school and he were still that geeky kid with braces who finally got a chance to make out with a cheerleader.

He made her feel like she was a gift that had been bestowed upon him, and as much as he wanted to tear the packaging off and play with his new toy, he continued to slowly unwrap the present and savor each moment of the reward.

The way he treated her was so different from the way Chad had. She and Chad had fallen in love as kids, barely out of high school. She couldn't see it then, but now she realized that he had always tried to make her feel like she was less than he was. It was always in subtle ways, but it took another man's attention to make Maggie realize the slights and appreciate that Jeremy didn't treat her that way.

Ugh. Chad. She just now realized that she hadn't told Jeremy about Chad staying at the house.

Jeremy slipped his hand under her blouse and ran his fingers along the bare skin of her back. Maggie arched into him, savoring his touch and the feel of his hand on her skin.

Now didn't really seem like the best time to tell him her ex had moved back home.

Maggie pulled her car into Sunny's driveway. It was the following Wednesday night, and she couldn't believe how fast the last week had flown. A big case at work was just finishing up and between that and worrying about Jeremy, her days this week had flown by in a blur.

Caught off guard at how quickly book club had rolled around again, she had stayed up late the night before, finishing the novel they were reading so she would be able to participate in tonight's book club meeting.

Edna lived a few houses down from Sunny, so Maggie assumed that she had already walked over. Cassie's car sat parked on the street, so she and Piper were most likely inside. Maggie took a deep breath, not sure if she was ready for the onslaught of questions about Jeremy and the impending murder case.

She hadn't seen Jeremy since the night she had dropped him at his house from the police station. They had talked on the phone, but each had spent the weekend and several nights the past week in their offices. Between her own busy caseload and the launch of Jeremy's new game, both of their plates were overflowing.

Knowing Jeremy had the added strain of the murder investigation and dealing with a company full of grief and questions, she tried to offer as much support as she could through texts and quick emails. As far as she knew, there had been no new word on Jim's murder case.

The topic of Chad had conveniently not come up, and she had yet to find a way to casually slip it into their conversation. She was trying not to face if that was purposeful on her part or not.

She knew she would have to face it tonight, though, with the Page Turners. There was no way they would let her skate by without telling them why he was still in the house. She wished she had an answer.

She knew he was there, but he had a way of making himself scarce when she got home from work. He was either tucked upstairs in Dylan's room watching television, or out of the house, most likely on the golf course. Although how he could still afford course fees when he was supposedly broke was beyond her.

He had been up last Wednesday night when she got home from Jeremy's, scaring the daylights out of her when she walked into the dark house. She had set her purse on the sofa and walked into the kitchen. The dim light above the sink was on, and Chad stood by the fridge wearing only a pair of pajama pants, holding a glass of milk and a handful of chocolate chip cookies.

She wasn't sure, but it seemed like he sucked in his stomach a little when she walked into the room. He did look good. He must have been working out to lose weight, because his stomach looked more toned and she couldn't see any of the flabby middle that he had been sporting the last five years of their marriage. He looked tanned and fit and younger. He looked more like the guy she had fallen in love with and spent years of her life with.

Hmm. Must be a trick of the light. Because that guy had left her for a new-and-improved model.

Chad set down the milk and leaned against the counter. "Hey. I heard you had a little excitement at book club tonight and you all ended up at the police station. So, did they arrest Super-Nerd?"

Maggie grimaced. Yeah, that was the guy she remembered. Chad had always had a way of putting down anything that he perceived as better than he was. "Come on, Chad. Don't do that."

"Sorry. You're right. Did they arrest Jeremy?" He held out a cookie, which she assumed was a peace offering. And it would taste better than an olive branch.

She sank onto the kitchen stool and took the cookie. "Of course they didn't arrest him. They just brought him in for questioning. It's his company. He's the best one to tell them what's going on there. I wish you wouldn't judge him when you don't even know him. He's really a great guy."

"Yeah? Does he make you happy?" Chad poured her a glass of milk and passed it across the counter. He acted as if the question were innocent, but seemed a little too eager for the answer.

"Yes. He does. And he's really good with the boys."

Chad appeared to bristle at the mention of their kids. "Is he over here a lot? Is he spending the night here?"

Whoa, buddy. "First of all, it's none of your business who's spending the night over here. But no, we're not at that stage yet. I'm not ready for anyone to be spending the night. In fact, I don't really want you spending the night here either. Speaking of which, how's the apartment hunting going? And by that I mean, when are you leaving?"

Chad laughed and slouched a little more against the counter, which Maggie recognized as the sign that he was about to lay on the charm, or bullshit, depending on which way you looked at it. "All right. You don't have to get all touchy about it. You just seem different. Not as tense. You look really good, actually. Like you're happier, and you smile more."

Yeah, well, she hadn't had a lot to smile about in those last few years with him. The fighting and cold shoulders had taken a lot of the fun out of their marriage. In the end, they had seemed more like roommates than lovers anyway.

She liked to stay up late working on case files, and Chad had taken to sleeping in the guest room stating that he didn't want his snoring to affect her sleep and that she could stay up later reading that way. As if he were doing her a favor by leaving their bed. Without even the accidental intimacy of sleeping in the same bed together, there came a point when she couldn't even remember the last time he had touched her.

Thinking about their marriage saddened her and then pissed her off. She thought it easier to just stop this train of thought now. "I am happier. But I'm also tired. See you in the morning." She slid off the stool, leaving the milk glass on the counter and headed for the stairs. She hadn't realized until later that night when she was brushing her teeth that he hadn't answered the question of when he was leaving.

🐾🐾

A screen door slammed, jarring Maggie back into the present.

She looked across to the neighboring house and saw that Jake had stepped out of the back door. He waved to her, and she assumed he must be heading to Sunny's as well. Probably for the dessert. What was it about cake that drew men out of the woodwork?

Time to face the music. She pushed the door open and met Jake halfway across the lawn. "Hey, Jake."

"Hey, Maggie. How's the lawyering business?" Jake grinned, and Maggie could see what drew Sunny to him. His skin carried the healthy glow of a summer tan, and his grin displayed gleaming white teeth. His one canine was just a little crooked, giving his smile just the right combination of charm and mischief. He wasn't as tall as Jeremy, but his shoulders were broad and muscular and he was drop-dead, head-turning gorgeous. No wonder Sunny walked around with a smile on her face all the time. She got to do the horizontal mambo with this hunk.

"It's good." They walked up Sunny's front walk to the porch.

Jake put a hand on the door but turned to Maggie before pulling it open. "How's Jeremy?"

Maggie stopped just short of running into him. "He's hanging in there. We've both been really busy this week, and I haven't had much of a chance to really talk to him."

"Did he tell you that he hired Finn and me to help figure out who murdered his employee?" Jake had taken an early retirement from the FBI, choosing instead to team up with Jerry Finney, an old friend who had a private investigation business. Sunny had told her that they'd mainly been doing a lot of background checks and some security work.

Maggie was surprised to hear that Jeremy had hired them and not told her. Although she knew Jeremy admired Jake, putting him up on a James Bond-style pedestal. It made sense that he would ask Jake for help if he was in trouble. "He hadn't told me yet, but I'm glad you're helping him. That's nice of you."

"Jeremy's a friend. I would've helped him anyway, but he made sure we knew this was a paid job. He said all of his resources were at our disposal. I'm just trying to figure out a reason to use his private helicopter." Jake laughed and pulled on the door, holding it open for her to walk in ahead of him.

Jeremy had a helicopter? She had never heard him mention that. Granted, he didn't talk much about his wealth. She wondered what else he'd been withholding.

"It's about time you got here." Piper met them at the door, throwing her arms around Maggie's middle in a hug. "Is Drew with you?"

Piper had been dating Maggie's son Drew all summer. She wasn't sure what would happen when the two left for college in the fall. "No, but he said he might drop by later to see you."

Piper grinned. "Probably because he heard we were ordering pizza." She led them into the kitchen, where Sunny, Cassie, and Edna sat around the table, an open pizza box in front of them. "I'll get you guys some plates."

Each woman stood to give Maggie a hug, and Beau, Sunny's golden retriever, gave her a welcoming sniff in the crotch. Feeling loved by her friends *and* by Beau, she sat at the table as Cassie passed her a warm slice of pizza.

Never one for subtlety, Edna peppered her with questions. "How's Jeremy? What's up with the investigation? What have they found out?"

"Settle down, Edna." Sunny held up a hand to her elderly neighbor. "Give the woman a minute to breathe."

Maggie shrugged. "I'm fine. I don't really know anything new. You should ask him." She pointed at Jake, who had forgone the plate and was standing at the counter, shoveling a piece of pizza into his mouth. "Jeremy just hired him to help with the investigation."

"What? Why?" Sunny looked at Jake, appearing as if this were news to her as well.

Jake finished chewing. "Look. Jeremy's a bright guy. He's just covering his bases. He's protecting himself and his company, in case the police try to come after him."

"Do they really think Jeremy is a suspect?" Cassie asked, a worried look on her face.

"I'm not sure. I think they're looking at everybody right now. It's their job. They have to look at the case from all angles." Jake picked up another piece of pizza. "I just wish he had a better alibi. Or any alibi, for that matter."

"Hold the phone. Jeremy doesn't have an alibi?" Edna looked over at Maggie. "I thought he was with you the night of the murder."

Maggie shook her head. She didn't want to admit it, but the fact that Jeremy had no alibi did make her uneasy. She was a lawyer, for heaven's sake, and that was the first thing they dug into. "He wasn't with me. He's been working on this new program, and he said he needed a night to stay home and work. He claimed he needed some quiet time to think and process through everything before things went live with his new game this week."

"So, don't they have at least an electronic trail to follow that shows him on the computer or making phone calls?" Edna asked. "I saw this detective show last week where they tracked the killer through his time spent on the internet."

Sunny nodded. "Yeah, I thought you guys liked to play some online game together. Can't they track his computer activity through the game?"

Maggie groaned. Normally, they spent several hours a night online together. Maggie wished she had pushed him to play that night. "We usually do, but not that night. He was completely unplugged. No phone, no computer. He said he just needed peace and quiet and that he spent the night in the pool and sitting in the hot tub."

"And unfortunately, no one can verify that," Jake added. "That's another reason he hired us."

"Who wants cupcakes?"

Maggie turned to see whose voice was coming from the front room, praying she was incorrectly identifying the deep baritone of her ex-husband.

Nope. Dead on. Drew walked into the kitchen, followed by his father. Chad was holding a pink box from her favorite bakery.

Chad set the box on the kitchen counter. "Hey, ladies. Drew said he was coming over to see Piper, and I thought I'd tag along and see how book club was going. I made him stop to pick up some treats on the way over." He looked at Maggie. "This is that bakery you like, right?"

Maggie stared daggers at her son.

Drew shrugged and shook his head. "Sorry, Mom. I didn't invite him. I just said I was headed over here, and he got in the car."

Edna stood and peeked under the bakery box lid. "Well, we don't like you, but we do like cake." She lifted a cupcake from the box, inhaling the scent of the decadent treat. Whipped chocolate frosting had been piped around the top of the cake, and a chocolate-covered coffee bean sat nestled in the center.

Jake held out his hand. "I don't think we've met. I'm Jake."

Maggie took a tiny, perverse pleasure in watching Jake squeeze Chad's hand. She could tell by the look on Chad's face that Jake was applying an added amount of pressure. "Jake, this is my ex-husband, Chad."

Chad pulled his hand free, flexing his fingers, but obviously determined not to show any weakness. "Pleased to meet you. I've heard a lot about you."

"Same here." Jake's voice held a measure of steeliness. Maggie could imagine him using that tone in an interrogation room, questioning a witness. He looked hard at Chad for an extra beat then pulled the lid back to examine the cupcake offering.

Reverting to the earlier reference to subtlety, Edna spoke up around a mouthful of cupcake. "So, Chad, how's the apartment hunting going? When are you gonna be moving out of Maggie's house?"

"Moving out? I wasn't aware that he moved in." The room suddenly became two sizes smaller and ten degrees warmer as Jeremy stood in the doorway of the kitchen holding a similar pink bakery box in his hands.

"Awkward." Edna turned to Maggie, a look of anticipation on her face.

"Edna, be quiet. You're not helping." Sunny passed her neighbor a napkin. "And you've got frosting on your nose."

Edna took the napkin. "What did I do? I'm just stating the obvious."

Chad stepped forward, his hand outstretched to Jeremy. "I'm Chad. I don't think we've met."

Jeremy stood still, his hands gripping the cake box, an icy quality to his voice. "I know who you are. But what are you doing here and why are you at Maggie's house? Aren't you supposed to be off having a midlife crisis with a convertible and a fake-boobed bimbo?"

"Good one." Edna raised her hand to high-five Jeremy, then lowered it at Sunny's look of disapproval.

Maggie crossed the room to Jeremy. She held out her arms to take the cake box and noticed a copy of their latest book club assignment on top of the box. She had an inner *awww* moment, then looked up at Jeremy. "You read the book?"

Jeremy passed her the box, and the paperback slid off and hit the floor with a thud. "Yeah, I did. I thought you would appreciate the effort of me thinking about you and doing something that you enjoy. But evidently, you didn't put out the same effort in thinking about me when you failed to mention that your ex-husband moved back in with you."

"He didn't move back in with me. He's just staying at the house for a few days." She realized that sounded weak, even to her own ears. Maggie reached for him, but he had already turned and was headed for the front door. "Jeremy, wait."

She turned back to the Page Turners, passing the cupcakes to Cassie. "I need to go after him. I'll call you guys later."

Sunny waved her on. "Go. Catch up to him. Call me later."

Maggie grabbed her purse and shot a look of anger at Chad before she hurried from the kitchen.

Jeremy was unlocking his car door.

"Wait. I want to talk to you." Maggie ran across the lawn to where he stood. She put her hand on his arm. "Jeremy, I'm sorry. I should have told you about Chad."

Jeremy shook his head. "Yes, you should have. He's been at your house for days. How could you not think this is information I'd like to know?"

"Well, you *have* had a lot going on."

"Don't lay this on me. You could have said something."

Maggie wasn't used to hearing anger in Jeremy's voice. At anyone, but especially not aimed at her. She was pretty sure they were having their first fight, on the street out in front of her best friend's house. She looked back at Sunny's house and saw the curtains drop back into place. She would place a hundred-dollar bet on the curtain-dropper's name being Edna.

She turned back to Jeremy. He looked angry and sad, and Maggie hated that she was the cause of those emotions. "You're right. I guess I was avoiding the situation. I was hoping if I ignored it, it would go away." She smiled at the weak joke aimed at Chad, hoping to lighten the situation.

Jeremy was not amused. He did not smile back. "So, what's the deal? Why is he back? Does he want to get back together with you?"

"No! Of course not." Maggie was stunned at the question. She hadn't even thought about that possibility. "He and Sapphire had a falling out. She apparently spent all of his money and then kicked him out. He didn't have any other place to stay."

"I can't believe you would let him stay with you."

"I can't believe it either. But Dylan was so glad to have his dad home. Our split has been really hard on the boys, and when I saw how happy it made him, I just caved. He's only staying for a few days. He didn't actually move back in."

"Then why did he show up here? And why did he bring you dessert?" The angry look crossed Jeremy's face again, and Maggie was sure he was thinking of the moment he walked in with the duplicate cake box.

"Who knows? I had no idea that he was coming. He rode over with Drew. He doesn't do surprises, though. He always has a motive." She hadn't considered that his motive could be winning her over. She pushed the ridiculous thought aside. "He probably wants to borrow money."

"He made me feel like an idiot. Like I was a geek in high school, trying to talk to the pretty girl and getting shown up by the cool jock once again."

Maggie moved closer, putting her arms around Jeremy's waist. "You are *not* an idiot. I love that you stopped by and brought us treats. And I will take brains over brawn any day of the week." The words brought back the hurt of Chad's desertion. She knew that he had resented her law degree and had claimed that she always acted like she was smarter than him. She'd always known she wanted to be a lawyer and had gone after her goal out of passion, not to prove that she had more intelligence.

Jeremy looked down at her and circled her back with his long arms. A crooked grin crossed his face. "I *did* read the book."

Maggie laughed. "Yes, you did. What'd you think?"

"It was terrible."

"Yeah, it was. It was Edna's pick."

"I figured." His voice trailed off as he leaned in and kissed her. His lips were soft against hers, but he pulled her tightly against him, his want evident in the pressure of his embrace.

Maggie kissed him back, her heart doing a little flip-flop that they had weathered their first argument and he still wanted her. Her body heated to his desire, and she reveled in the stomach-fluttering feeling of excitement his kisses brought her. She never thought she would experience another "first kiss" moment or have that nervous-exciting feeling about holding someone's hand.

She had dated a few other guys, but most of them just made her mad. The way they walked or talked or chewed their food. Pretty much everything about most men made her mad. That was why she was surprised by her reaction to Jeremy. She truly enjoyed his company. She liked talking to him and spending time with him. And she *really* liked kissing him.

Wouldn't it be just her luck to finally find a guy she liked and he turned out to be a murderer?

Maggie pulled into Jeremy's driveway behind his 4Runner. They'd gone back into Sunny's house for a few minutes, then he invited her back to his place for a glass of wine. She had begged out of book club for the night and Piper had readily followed suit, claiming she had tons to do to finish filling out her college applications. Jeremy had offered to look them over for her after she was done.

Maggie loved the way Jeremy got along with her closest friends. His offer to help Piper made her a little gooey inside. Plus he brought her favorite treats and acted like he genuinely wanted to participate in the book club.

She still couldn't believe that he had read the book. Before they left the house, he and Edna had gotten into a feverish debate over the symbolism of the main character's final choice in the book. Maggie smiled at the memory of how he so easily charmed Edna. He had told her that he and his brother grew up with just their mom. She guessed being raised by a single mother taught you a few things about how to treat women.

Maggie climbed from her car and met him at the front door. She waited while he unlocked the door and held it open for her to enter first. What a gentleman. Maybe Edna wasn't the only one being swayed by his charm.

Jeremy reached an arm around her and flipped the light switch. Light filled the room, and Maggie gasped in shock.

The front room had been totally ransacked! The sofa was ripped, and stuffing lay spread out across the floor. The rugs were pulled back, and an armchair was overturned. Magazines previously arranged artfully on the coffee table were now shredded to bits and pieces, flung from one side of the room to another.

Maggie stared at the destruction in horror. "Oh my gosh, Jeremy! What happened? Who could have done this?" Her mind immediately went to Jim's murder. "It looks like someone was searching for something. Could this be connected to Jim?"

"I don't see how." Jeremy stood gaping at his destroyed living room, a look of stunned disbelief on his face. "I don't know what they thought they would find here. I don't have anything to hide."

"Well, someone obviously thinks you do."

The sound of heavy furniture being moved across the floor came from the next room. Maggie grabbed for Jeremy's arm. "They must still be here," she whispered. "What should we do?"

Jeremy pushed her behind him, shielding her with his body. "They must not have heard us come in. Let's go back outside, and we'll call the police."

Before they could take a step backward, an overturned armchair appeared in the doorway. It moved forward with a loud scrape against the hardwood floor as it was pushed into the room.

Jeremy fumbled around him, grabbing an umbrella from the stand by the door to use as a weapon. He brandished it like a sword, and Maggie held her breath as they waited for the culprit to appear. She was too frightened to even comment on Jeremy's umbrella-fighting skills.

The armchair moved another six inches into the room and their assailant appeared behind it, pushing the chair forward with his large, furry snout.

"Chewie!" They said his name at the same time and the dog looked up, then bounded toward them, a look of pure joy at their presence. He jumped up on Jeremy, almost knocking him off his feet.

The massive dog ran in a circle around them. He gave Maggie's crotch a quick sniff, then ran around the room, flinging stuffing from the sofa cushion in the air as if he were showing off his accomplishments and inviting them to play with him.

"Holy destruction. I can't believe one dog could do this in only a few hours." Jeremy looked around in bewilderment.

Maggie laughed. "I'm just thankful it wasn't an intruder." She nudged the umbrella with her foot. "Although it was pretty hot how you were ready to defend me with an umbrella-sword."

"Yeah? Did you like that?" He held the umbrella out in front of him, chopping the air with wide strokes. "*En garde.*"

Chewie loved this new game and barked loudly, racing back and forth across the living room, skidding on the loose rug and rolling into the overturned chair.

He scrambled to his feet and raced into the kitchen, running circles around the center island.

Jeremy trailed the dog into the kitchen. "Come back here, you scoundrel, and fight like a man." He ran around the kitchen island in full chase, but stopped short as he came around the far side of the counter. "Oh, crap! Maggie, you better come in here."

Maggie followed slowly, hesitant to see what had grabbed Jeremy's attention. She peeked around the counter to see the trash can overturned and the floor covered in food and garbage. "Oh, gross. I didn't need to see that." She laughed. "You just went from knight to servant in two seconds flat. I hope you have some rubber gloves."

"It's not that." Jeremy's face held a serious expression. "I had a rotisserie chicken in the trash and there's only the wrapper left. That dog must have eaten that whole chicken carcass."

"So?"

"So, dogs aren't supposed to eat chicken bones. They can splinter and puncture their insides and they can die." Jeremy paled at the implication.

Maggie looked over at the mutt. He had grabbed some of the garbage as he ran by and stood by the kitchen table, holding a milk carton in his mouth. "He looks all right to me."

"We've got to get him to a doctor. Now." He ran for the front door, calling for the dog. Chewie ran after him, still playing the fun chase game. Jeremy stopped and turned to her. "I don't even have a vet. Do you have a vet? How do we find a vet? Should we Google one? Do they have hours this late? What should we do? I don't want him to die."

Maggie crossed the room and put her arms around him. "You're so cute when you're in crisis." She leaned up and kissed him on the cheek. "Grab his collar. Of course I have a vet. And they have urgent-care hours, just like humans do. I programmed the number in my phone after Barney had a run-in with a coyote and had to get stitches in his leg."

She reached for the front door. "Hand me your keys. I'll drive, but we're taking your car."

Thirty minutes later, they sat in an examining room waiting for the doctor to come in. Jeremy had used the time on the drive over to place two calls. One to his housekeeper, to please come in early the next day to take care of the mess and to order replacement furniture.

And the other to the contractor who had installed his basketball court. He explained the situation and was assured they could have a temporary, but sturdy, dog run built in the back yard within a couple of days.

Hmm. Maggie didn't see Jeremy ever flaunt his money, but when he needed something done, evidently he had people to get things done for him. Must be nice to have people. Or at least the money to have people, if you needed them.

They had been the only ones at the emergency clinic, and the vet tech had shown them into a room and taken Chewie's vitals. The dog was not overjoyed at having his temperature taken with a rectal thermometer—but then, nobody usually was. At least Chewie got a treat for his discomfort. He gobbled down the dog biscuit as if he were still hungry after the can of trash and the living room furniture he had eaten earlier.

Jeremy paced back and forth across the small room. Chewie lay on the floor, his eyes tracking his new master as he moved around the room.

The door opened and the veterinarian entered, sticking his hand out in greeting. "Hello, I'm Dr. Holliday." He shook Jeremy's hand, then bent to stroke the big dog's head. "Wow. You're a big fella, aren't you? What's going on with this guy?"

Jeremy explained how they had found the house when they arrived home and the missing contents of the scattered trash. "I'm sure he ate an entire chicken carcass, and most likely, some of the stuffing out of my sofa."

The vet laughed. "That doesn't surprise me. You want to help me get him on the table, and we'll see what's going on?" Together, they lifted the dog onto the table and the vet gave him a thorough examination.

Jeremy watched every move, worry in his eyes. "Is he going to be all right? Will he die?"

Maggie was touched by the concern Jeremy had for this dog already. He hadn't even seemed angry about the dog having his living room for supper. She had even heard him laughing about it as he talked with his contractor.

Chad would never have acted like that. She remembered when Barney was a puppy and had chewed up one of Chad's slippers. Chad had been so angry, he'd yelled at the poor dog for two days. She couldn't imagine what would have happened if he'd eaten their sofa. But Jeremy took it all in stride, more worried about the dog's digestive system than his furniture. One more reason why she was falling for this man. And one more reason that made it harder for her to see him as a murderer.

Dr. Holliday finished his exam and patted Chewie's side. "I think he's going to be fine. The whole thing with chicken bones is something that can happen, but is more common with smaller breeds. This guy is so big, he could probably eat an ostrich carcass and be fine. A lot of these big dog breeds are used as hunting dogs, and they've been known to swallow ducks practically whole." He scribbled on a little pad and passed the sheet to Jeremy. "Here's a little something for his digestion if he seems to have an upset stomach. But really, he probably won't show any signs of discomfort at all. If you notice he's not eating or pooping, check back in with me."

Jeremy took the dog's leash as the doctor closed the door behind him. "Well, so far he hasn't had trouble with either." He smiled at Maggie, a look of relief on his face. "I guess he's going to be okay. Let's take this big mutt and get out of here."

Maggie stepped onto the soccer field and right into a mud puddle. It was Friday night, and the gritty mud was indicative of how the rest of her day had gone. Her assistant had lost an important file, her lunch order had been wrong, and she'd broken a nail. Her one bright spot was getting to watch Dylan's game tonight and knowing Jeremy would be here.

She hadn't seen him since the cupcake fiasco earlier in the week. They had talked on the phone the night before, but they were each busy and their conversations had been brief. He had told her Chewie seemed to be doing fine and was enjoying the new dog run, and the new furniture was expected to be delivered Friday afternoon.

He said that he would come to Dylan's soccer game. She looked anxiously over at the bleachers for his dark hair, her heart racing a little in anticipation.

Oh, crud. Her heart sank at the dark-haired man she did see. No Jeremy, but Chad-the-Cheater was sitting center row, next to Drew and Piper. And the only open spot on the bleacher was next to Chad. She walked over to the stands, wiping her shoe on the grass as she went.

She flopped down on the bench, leaving space for Jeremy on one side and as much room between her and Chad as she could manage.

Her ex-husband smiled and passed her a cold can of Diet Coke. "Hey, Maggie-May. Rough day at the office?"

"Yes, as a matter of fact, it was." She hated that he could still read her so easily. She did take the can of soda, though. "And I told you not to call me that."

"Sorry. Just trying to be thoughtful."

As if. Who was this guy? He hadn't given a thought to anyone but himself in years. "What are you doing here anyway? You didn't come to that many games when we were married. Why show up now?"

"Ouch." He faked a shot to the chest. "Drew called me and said he couldn't get Dylan picked up and asked me to bring him over. I wasn't busy, so I said I would. I promised Dylan we could go to that new burger place down on 8th Street after the game. Wanna join us?"

"She's got plans." Jeremy slid into the bleachers on Maggie's other side, sliding his arm around her waist and laying a quick, but proprietary, kiss on her lips.

Maggie shrugged. "Sorry, I've got plans." She turned to Jeremy, a smile on her just-kissed lips. "Hey, how was your day?"

"Crazy. We're in the midst of this huge launch, and yet we're all grieving for Jim. It's hard because we have so much to do, and we all have to work together, but there's this weird undertone of suspicion around the office. I don't know what I would have done without Charlotte. She's put in a ton of extra hours and really been there for me this week."

"I bet she has," Maggie muttered. Before she could say more, the action on the field started, and she got lost in watching her son play soccer.

The hour and a half flew by, and their team won, with Dylan scoring two goals and making an assist. The group hung out by the concession stand waiting for Dylan to finish with the team.

Piper stood holding hands with Drew. She did her best to break the awkward silence. "So, Maggie, we're gonna try book club again tomorrow morning at your house, right?"

Maggie cringed. She applauded the effort at conversation, but wished Piper would not have brought up the uncomfortable memory of book club and the double cupcake deliveries. She also wished she hadn't drunk that second can of soda. "I'll be right back."

As much as she hated to use the soccer field's Porta-Potty, she was desperate. She squeezed through the door and quickly did her business, trying not to touch anything in the little green cubicle. A dispenser of hand sanitizer clung to the wall, and she squeezed a glob of the clear slimy liquid into her hand.

Maggie jumped as her cell phone vibrated. She reached in her back pocket to pull the phone free, and knocked her elbow against the side wall of the Porta-Potty. The sanitizer had made her hands just slick enough that she lost her grip and bobbled the phone before it dropped into the murky blue water two feet below.

Shit! Literally. *Are you kidding?* What was happening to her? She had never dropped a phone in the toilet in her life, and now she had lost two in the last two weeks. She either needed to chain them to her belt-loop or stop using outside toilets. She voted for the latter.

She slammed the door of the porta-john open and stepped out with a curse. "I dropped my F-ing phone down the toilet again! It's my new one that I just replaced. I'm so mad!"

"Oh no. That sucks." Piper laughed. "But it's also kind of funny."

"Hi, Mom. Did you see my goals?" Dylan loped up to the group and hugged his mother. He pulled back and must have recognized her angry face. "What's wrong? Did Dad do something?"

Maggie shook her head and hugged her son again. "No. It's not your dad. This time. I just dropped my damn phone down the toilet."

"Wait. I got it." The green door of the Porta-Potty opened and Chad emerged, proudly holding her phone aloft. His hand and part-way up his wrist were stained blue from the chemically treated water of the Porta-Potty.

Oh. No. He didn't.

Maggie felt the bile rise in her throat as Chad extended his blue-stained hand to her, the phone pinched between his fingers. "Oh, my gosh, Chad. I am NOT touching that! Just throw it away."

"What? You were so bummed you lost it. I thought I was helping you." His face took on the pitiful, sad look of a shamed puppy.

"Look at your hand."

Chad shrugged. "It's just water. They put so many chemicals in it, it's practically like sticking your hand in a swimming pool. I'm sure it'll wash right off."

"Dad, that is disgusting." Drew held his hand over his mouth and pushed the park's trash- can toward his dad with his foot. "Throw it away."

"It's an iPhone. And it's new." Chad forlornly dropped the cell phone into the trash-can.

"And I bought the insurance," Maggie said.

"Hey, I was just trying to help." Chad did not like being the butt of any joke, and it seemed he realized his act of chivalry was quickly turning into a comedic gag.

Maggie watched his face and recognized the expression of anger that was beginning to simmer just under the surface. "Thank you for the effort, Chad. I appreciate it." She turned to Jeremy. "I think we're going to go."

She gave her son one more quick squeeze. "You played a great game, honey. Have fun getting dinner with your dad. We'll see you later."

Maggie and Jeremy curled together on the new sofa in Jeremy's living room. His housekeeper had pulled off a miracle, and the room looked good as new.

Maggie popped a piece of popcorn in her mouth. They had just finished watching a movie and were talking about Dylan's game.

"Maybe you should check on Chad." Jeremy tried to hold in his laughter. "He seemed so sad when we left. I don't want him to be *blue*."

Maggie playfully punched Jeremy in the arm. He burst into a fit of laughter as he cracked another *blue* joke at Chad's expense. "Enough already."

Jeremy took a deep breath, trying to get himself under control. "Sorry, that just came on, out of the blue." Another burst of laughter.

Maggie gave him her best stern mom/lawyer look.

"Okay. No, really. I'll stop." Jeremy positioned his face into a sober expression. "I've just been laughing until I'm blue in the face. Or the hand." More chuckling.

Maggie tried to keep a straight face. His laughter was infantile, but still contagious. "Come on. You have to run out of these eventually."

"Oh, I could go all night." He wiggled his eyebrows, grinning at the double meaning.

Maggie got the message too and promptly changed the subject. "I still can't believe he fished that phone out of there. I just don't know why he would do that. Why *anyone* would do that."

"Really, Maggie?" Jeremy's tone sobered. "We all know why he did it. He's trying to win you back."

Could that be true? Thinking back on the past few weeks, it seemed like he had been trying to be extra thoughtful. She thought he was trying to impress the boys, but maybe he was doing it for her. "I don't think so. He had me once and he threw me away."

"His loss was my gain." Jeremy rubbed his hand along her spine. "Sometimes it takes losing something to realize how great you actually had it."

Maggie didn't think things had been that great the last few years. In fact, she had to think really hard to when things had been even good. Wait. Why was she spending time thinking about the past when her future could be sitting right next to her, massaging her back? She couldn't think of a time when Chad had ever rubbed her back. She was always the one giving to him. And he was always the taker.

She wanted something different with Jeremy. Something more. She loved the way he wanted to touch her, like she was a treasure that he had found. He held her in such regard, like he valued her and couldn't believe that she was with him. Chad acted like she should consider herself lucky to be with him.

She looked up at Jeremy. His dark brown eyes held such sincerity. She wanted to believe in him. To trust him. With her body. With her heart.

She watched his eyes change and take on a look of desire as the hand that was rubbing her back slid around her waist and pulled her against him.

He leaned his forehead against hers. "Your expression just turned serious. What are you thinking about, Maggie?"

She smiled, glad they weren't playing poker. "I was thinking about us. I'm not very good at this relationship thing. Evidently, I don't inspire men to stick around."

"Stop it. I hate that that bastard made you feel less about yourself." He brought his hand up and laid it against her cheek. "I can't believe that a woman like you would even consider falling for a nerdy guy like me. Maggie, I know we haven't been dating for a long time, but something about you just clicks with me. And I plan on staying around for as long as you'll have me."

She wanted to believe him. But something inside of her held back. Afraid to trust again.

Jeremy tipped her chin up to look at him. He ran his thumb along her bottom lip. "You are an amazing woman, Maggie. You're smart and beautiful."

Maggie closed her eyes and took a deep breath, hesitant to share her inner-most thoughts. The feel of his thumb touching her lip sent delicious shivers down her spine. Her body heated, wanting him, craving him. But not just with her body. She wanted his heart as well.

She opened her eyes, peering at Jeremy through her lashes, praying that her confessions would be heard with understanding. "But smart and beautiful aren't enough. *I* wasn't enough."

Jeremy's grip on her back tightened and his voice choked with emotion. "You are *more* than enough for me. I think about you every day, Maggie. Every minute of every day. I think about what I can do to prove I am worthy of you. Of what I can do to make you happy. I think about what I can do to make your face break out into that amazing smile that you have just for me. I would do just about anything for that smile."

Maggie's heart ached with tenderness for this man who opened himself up to her. Who shared his thoughts and his feelings. "I think about you too."

Jeremy dipped his head to lightly touch her lips with his. He kissed her then pulled back. "I don't just think about you, Maggie. I think about being with you." He kissed her again. "I think about kissing you and touching you." Another kiss, this one more urgent, filled with the desire of which he spoke. "I need you, Maggie. I want you. I want you so bad."

She had spent so many years in an emotional wasteland, she wasn't sure if this man was really an oasis or just a mirage. Something that looked beautiful, but wavered in the sun and disappeared if you got too close. There was only one way to find out. She had to get close enough to see if it was real. She had to dip her toe in the water to see if it would bring blessed relief. If this man was an illusion or something real, something she had been searching for.

She gave in to her desire and kissed him back. Kissed him with abandon, with the carnal need that swelled inside of her. She wanted his hands on her, touching her, caressing her body.

He pulled her under him on the sofa, his body heavy on hers. His hands thrust into her hair, cradling her head as he feasted on her mouth, her neck, her chest.

Sinking into the leather sofa, she wrapped her legs around him. She welcomed the weight of him on top of her, gripping his lean and muscled arms as he trailed his lips along her neck. He pushed up, using one hand to steady himself and the other to flick the buttons of her blouse open, one achingly slow button at a time. With each button he unfastened, he leaned down and left a kiss along her skin where the button had been.

She arched up against him, relishing the anticipation of each button as his lips touched her most sensitive spots. She gasped as he kissed the dip between her breasts, the lace of her bra peeking out of the loosened blouse. Another button, a kiss, then another button. His fingers brushed her skin as he pulled the fabric apart and laid his mouth against her stomach, circling her belly button with his tongue. The last button freed and her shirt lay completely open, exposing her skin to him.

He trailed a line of kisses along the waistband of her pants, cupping her bottom with his free hand. His touch set her on fire. She was about to come as undone as the buttons on her blouse.

She gripped his head, his hair soft under her fingers. It had been so long since she had been touched with such longing from a man. The desire in her body rivaled with the desire of her heart. She wanted this man. All of him. His body, his heart, his soul.

Jeremy pulled back, standing up next to the sofa and looking down on her. "You are so beautiful." He leaned over and slid his arms under her, lifting her from the sofa and cradling her against him. He looked into her eyes. "I'm taking you to my bed. Are you okay with that?"

Holy hot fantasies. She thrilled at the thought of him carrying her to his bedroom. Jeremy was usually so gentle with her, her heart raced at this more forceful side of him. The strength in his grip on her made her feel as if she weighed nothing. The power of the moment had her afraid to speak. She could only lose herself in his eyes and nod her head.

That nod was all he needed. He leaned in to indulge her lips once more, his kiss a preview of the passion to come. Then he carried her to his bed.

The smell of bacon filled the air the next morning as Maggie stepped out of her bedroom, calling to her like the siren song of breakfast food. Yawning, she stumbled down the stairs, not prepared to see Sunny, Maggie, and Edna sitting in her living room.

Edna waggled a thumb in her direction. "Looks like Sleeping Beauty finally decided to get up. Somebody have a late one last night?"

Sometimes Edna was hard to take, even *after* she'd had coffee. But she was almost impossible pre-caffeine. "What are you guys doing here?"

"We're here for book club," Sunny said. "Remember we rescheduled to this morning. You are really out of it."

It was coming back to her now. "Of course. Sorry. I got in late last night."

"Late like midnight?" Cassie asked.

"Late like three or four."

"In the morning?" Cassie looked skeptically at her friend. "What were you doing till three or four in the morning?"

Maggie smiled.

And Edna knew. She let out a naughty cackle. "You were out last night *doing* it!"

"Doing what?" Sometimes it took Cassie a few minutes to catch up.

"It!" Edna explained. "The mattress mambo, getting down and dirty, playing hide the sausage, getting a booty call, getting the hot beef injection, punching the monkey."

"Enough." Sunny swatted at Edna. "We get the picture."

"Punching the monkey?" Cassie looked questioningly at Edna. "What does that even mean?"

Edna shrugged. "I don't know. I heard it on the radio."

"The point is. You did *it*." Sunny pointed at Maggie's messy hair. "And from the looks of your hair, *it* must have been pretty good."

Maggie tried her best to glare at her friends, but couldn't hold the frown. Plus, she felt too dang good. A smile broke out across her face. "Okay. I did spend some 'quality time' with Jeremy last night." She waved a hand in Edna's direction. "But there were no monkeys involved. Getting punched or otherwise."

Cassie clapped her hands together. "Yay. This means you must like him. You really like him, don't you, Maggie?"

Why were her friends so lovable and so annoying at the same time? She really needed caffeine. And from the comment Sunny aimed at her hair, she must need a shower as well. "Yes, I really like him. Now quit talking about it and somebody please find me a cup of coffee. I need ten minutes to take a quick shower, then I'll be back down to talk about the book we read or about the weather or about Edna's bunion. But I do not want to talk about Jeremy or a hot beef injection, for heaven's sake." She shook her head, muttering to herself as she walked back up the stairs. "Where does she come up with this stuff?"

Twenty minutes later, Maggie walked in to the kitchen feeling fresher and much happier. She wore a pair of khaki shorts and a white V-neck t-shirt and had quickly brushed on a little shadow and mascara. Her hair was long and loose, falling straight down her back, still damp after only a quick zap with the hairdryer.

One of her friends had slipped a cup of coffee onto the bathroom counter while she was in the shower. She now had clean hair *and* caffeine. The only thing that could ruin her mood was the man standing behind her counter holding a bowl full of waffle batter.

Chad hefted the bowl at her. "Hey Maggie-May. You're just in time. I made breakfast."

He slid a fresh waffle onto a plate, the edges crisp and golden brown. Passing her the plate, her eyes widened at the vividly blue-stained skin of Chad's hand and wrist.

Edna waved a fork in the air, talking around her bite. "I still think he's an A-hole, but Papa Smurf there makes some pretty dang good waffles."

Oh. My. Gosh. She did not just go there. Maggie turned to the table, reaching for the syrup to mask the smile on her face. She stuffed a bite of waffle in her mouth to keep the giggles from bubbling out. "Good waffles."

"Thanks. Did you get the coffee I brought you?" He gestured to the empty mug with his blue-tainted hand. "Pass me your cup, and I'll get you a refill."

What? He brought her the coffee? Did that mean he came in the bathroom while she was showering?

She carried her cup around the center island, preferring to fill the mug herself. "We need to discuss some boundaries."

Chad shrugged. "We were married for eighteen years. It's not like I haven't seen it before."

"What? You looked?" Maggie reached for the coffeepot, squeezing in behind Chad and trying not to brush against him.

He inhaled deeply. "Geez. You still smell amazing."

"You realize we're all in the room and we can hear you?" Piper said.

Maggie turned to see Piper sitting at the kitchen table, grinning at her over a plate holding a giant waffle drowning in dark pools of syrup. "When did you get here?"

"I've been here. I rode over with Cassie. I was talking to Drew before he left for work."

"How did the college apps go last night?"

"Good. Cassie stayed up with me. She was working on her coupons and another one of those contest entries."

Cassie was always entering contests, sending in recipes and entry forms for sweepstakes and free samples. She licked her fork and pointed it at her niece. "Hey, somebody has to win those things. It could just as easily be me."

"Which schools are you looking at, Piper?" Maggie asked, used to Cassie's claims of winning the next big sweepstakes.

"Only three. The two big in-state universities and the local community college. Obviously, I'm hoping to get into the same school as Drew."

Maggie smiled at the girl. She had changed so much from when she had first come to live with Cassie. She had been a moody, depressed teenager, wearing dark clothes and makeup and taking out her anger with sarcasm at everyone around her. "I'm really proud of you. I'll keep my fingers crossed for you."

"Thanks. I'm not sure I have the grades to get in. Before I moved here, I would never have dreamed that I could even get into college. You all have really helped me to believe in myself. Now, I know this is what I really want and that I can make it happen."

Before Maggie could reply to the girl's sweet sentiment, the doorbell rang.

She filled her cup and carried her coffee into the living room to answer the door. Maggie couldn't imagine who would be here this early on a Saturday. Most of her sons' friends didn't get out of bed until noon on the weekends.

Taking a sip from her cup, she opened the door, and almost spat her coffee out. "What are you doing here?"

Nothing could have prepared her for the sight of Officer McCarthy standing on her doorstep, wearing a leather jacket, Aviator sunglasses, and heavy black motorcycle boots. She looked behind him to the gleaming black and silver Harley-Davidson that sat parked in her driveway.

Arching an eyebrow, she looked at him questioningly. "Are you here to offer me a ride on your bike?"

He pulled the sunglasses off, and a smile replaced the serious look on Mac's face. "If I said yes, would you accept?"

Maggie heard the challenge in his voice, almost as if he were daring her to hop on his motorcycle and ride off with him. Considering the scene she would be leaving behind in her kitchen, she was actually tempted to say yes. She shook her head. "Not today."

"Hmm. Not today or not at all?" He gave her another grin, and she was dazzled by the pearly white of his teeth.

She had thought he looked good in his cop uniform, but Holy Cow, he was downright dreamy in jeans and the muscle-hugging black t-shirt he wore under the leather jacket. The fantasy part of her brain went to a vision of him in motorcycle chaps, but she shook her head to clear the thought. He was just so buff and so tall. He was easily six-four, and being tall herself, she liked the way he made her feel small as she stood barefoot, looking up at him.

Geez. Down, girl. She needed to get back on track here.

As a lawyer and a woman, she was well practiced in the art of changing the subject. "What are you doing here, Officer McCarthy? I don't imagine this is just a social call."

"Please, call me Mac. And no, it isn't just a social call. Although I kind of wish it was." He looked out across her yard, and when he turned back to her, his face wore the stern expression of someone carrying bad news.

All of a sudden, Maggie wanted to shut the door, pretend this hadn't happened, go back to bed, stay under the covers all day, and not answer the door to this good-looking police officer and his motorcycle. But she was never one to run from trouble. She would rather face it head on and stare it down. "All right. What is it?"

"It's about Jeremy. We've got some new information, and it doesn't look good for him."

"Why are you telling me?"

"That's a really great question." Mac sighed and ran a hand over his clean-shaven bald head. "Maybe simply because I like you."

Maggie gulped and took a sip of her now lukewarm coffee.

"And because it's a small town and information tends to leak easily. Especially to your bunch. It wouldn't surprise me if that Edna has a police scanner next to her bed."

She laughed softly, still uneasy about the information he was about to share. "So, if I was going to hear it anyway, why not let me hear it from them?"

"Because I wanted you to hear it from me. So you would believe it. And not just think it was a rumor."

Uh oh. Every nerve in Maggie's body went on full alert. This was going to be bad. She took a deep breath. "Well, tell me."

"First of all, we checked out Jim's bank account, and a few things stood out. A few very large things. Within the last month, he made two notable deposits.

One was a wire for twenty-five thousand dollars that we traced to Jeremy's competitor, SkyVision. And the other was a ten- thousand-dollar check from Jeremy himself."

Maggie thought for a minute. "Both deposits could be easily explained. Maybe Jeremy offered him a bonus. They'd been working really hard on this new game."

"Maybe. But that wouldn't explain the wire transfer from the company that has every reason to want to steal that new game."

Which would also add up to a big fat motive for Jeremy. "But still, this is all circumstantial. If Jeremy found out Jim were selling secrets to his rival, why not just fire him? He certainly wouldn't have to kill him."

This information wasn't so bad. Certainly not worth all the dramatic buildup. Maggie had a bad feeling there was more coming.

"There's more," Mac said.

She knew it. Sometimes she hated it that she was always right. She stared at Mac. Daring him to destroy her with his next words.

"Jeremy lied about his alibi."

The breath went out of her lungs. This could be bad. If she didn't ask, maybe he wouldn't tell her. "Where was he?"

"Charlotte came forward last night and admitted that the two of them spent the night in a motel together. She's got a receipt from the Travel Inn, and the desk clerk remembers her checking in with a dark-haired guy."

Maggie felt like she had been punched in the stomach. Not Jeremy. Not the man that she had given herself to the night before. The one who had touched her and spoke words of love into her ear. Not the man who had laughed off those too-personal-sounding texts from his coworker. "That can't be true."

"I'm sorry, Maggie."

"That bastard!"

Maggie jumped at Edna's voice. She closed her eyes. *Please no.* Turning around, she opened her eyes and saw the Page Turners standing in the living room behind her. The stunned expressions on their faces told her that they had heard everything. Her heart sank even further as she saw Chad leaning against the jam of the kitchen doorway, a spatula still in his hand.

She turned back to Mac, praying that he had no more information for her. She had been humiliated enough for one day. For one week. For one year. "Anything else?"

Mac shook his head. "We're still digging. I really am sorry. And I'm sorry that I had to be the one to tell you."

"It doesn't matter who told me. It doesn't change it." She put her hand on the door. "Thanks for letting me know."

He took a step backward. "You know where to find me, if you need anything."

She shut the front door, leaning heavily against it. If she needed anything. Yes, she needed something. She needed this day to go away. She needed to go back to that great feeling she had getting out of bed this morning. She needed Jeremy to not have lied. To not have slept with another woman. To not have paid off the murder victim.

She needed a lot of things. But mainly, she needed her new boyfriend to not be a murderer.

"Soooo, that happened." Maggie sat on the sofa, looking at her closest friends and trying not to cry in front of them. She always held such a tough exterior, but inside she was crumbling like a house made of sand.

Cassie sat on the sofa next to her and gently rubbed her back. "I can't believe it."

Sunny sat on her other side, forming a protective shield around Maggie. "I wouldn't have believed it if Mac hadn't shown up to tell us himself."

"That's why he did. He knew you wouldn't believe him otherwise." Edna sat across from them, her bony bottom perched on the side of the loveseat, the opposite of Piper, who curled casually into the corner of the small sofa. "So, the question is, what are you gonna do about it?"

Maggie covered her face with her hands. "I don't know."

"I could make you another waffle." Chad waved the spatula, still standing in the doorway of the kitchen.

"Shut up, Chad. You're not helping." Maggie leaned back. "I guess I'll go talk to him. Confront him and give him a chance to tell me his side of the story."

Edna popped up from her seat. "Okay. We'll all go. I have a few questions I would like to ask him, too."

"That's okay. I don't need to bring my entire posse with me, like I'm afraid to face him on my own." Although Maggie *was* afraid. In fact, she was terrified.

Sunny took Maggie's hand, holding it gently in hers, the pressure helping to ease the trembling. "I have an idea. Why don't we just give you a ride over? We'll stay in the car and if you need us, great. If not, you can give us the signal, and we'll take off, and Jeremy can drive you home later."

Maggie thought for a second. This did not seem like a completely terrible idea.

"I'm not staying in the car," Edna said, already hefting her purse onto her shoulder.

Cassie gave her a stern "mom" look. "Yes. You are. Or you're not coming along." She stood up, reaching for her bag and giving orders. "I'll drive. We can all fit in the minivan. Maggie, go find some shoes and make sure you brush your teeth. Sunny, you grab her purse. Piper, grab some chips."

Maggie and Sunny looked at her questioningly on the last instructions.

Cassie looked back innocently. "What? We might get hungry."

"How 'bout me? Can I come?" Chad asked.

"No!" The five women's voices joined in a chorus of one word.

Thirty minutes later, the Pleasant Valley Page Turners sat in Cassie's van, parked a few houses away from Jeremy's.

At Cassie's advice, Maggie had thrown on some flip-flops and brushed her teeth. The mundane task had calmed her a little, but the drive over had given her nerves plenty of time to rev back up into supernova mode.

She looked at her cohorts. Piper was in the far back seat, one earbud tucked in her ear, listening to music and the women talking while simultaneously staring out the window. Sunny and Edna sat in the middle seat, wearing matching expressions of support. Cassie had already pushed the driver's seat back and reached for the chips, ready to settle in for the wait.

"Thanks, you guys. I'm glad you came with me." Maggie smiled at her friends. "But I've changed my mind. Let's forget this dumb idea and go see a movie. We can gorge ourselves on popcorn with tons of butter and pretend this never happened."

"Yum. Popcorn does sound good." Edna leaned forward. "I heard there's a new movie out with Hugh Jackman, and he barely wears a shirt the whole movie."

Sunny waved Edna back into the seat. "We are not going to a movie. You can do this. You are Maggie Hayes, attorney-at-law, and a mother. You have a law degree, and you have given birth. You are one tough chick. You can do this."

Maggie appreciated the pep talk, though was not exactly sure how being a lawyer and motherhood correlated with each other. But still, Sunny was right. She could do this.

She dug in her purse for her favorite lip gloss. Turning the rearview mirror, she quickly swiped on a dab of color, then popped a stick of spearmint gum in her mouth. She was as ready as she was gonna get. She nodded at the Page Turners and pushed the van door open.

She walked quickly up the sidewalk, determined to face Jeremy. Do it quick. Like ripping off a Band-Aid. But, as she got closer to the house, she saw that the front door stood ajar. She approached the door cautiously, tiptoeing up the front steps.

She reached her hand out to the open door, both praying that Jeremy was okay and reprimanding herself for doing something so stupid. If the heroine did this in the movies, Maggie was always the first one to yell at her to run away. Go get help. Call the police.

Yeah, and tell them what? "Hi, I went over to confront my boyfriend for cheating on me, and his front door was open. Send the cops fast!"

This was ridiculous. But she was also smart. She was turning to head back to the van to get the girls to come in with her when she heard Jeremy's voice. He must have been standing in the living room, because she could hear him speaking clearly.

"Look, I'm about ready to head up and see if I can find anything out."

No one answered, so Maggie deduced he must be on the phone. Wow, she was quite the detective. See, that law degree was really paying off.

"I understand that, Charlotte. I'll meet you there as soon as I can."

Charlotte?! He was meeting Charlotte? Where? What for? She leaned her head closer to the door, listening attentively.

"All right. See you soon." He paused. "You too. Bye."

Maggie stood up straight. Crap! She needed to get out of there. She turned and sprinted toward the van, her stupid sandals slapping the sidewalk with each step.

She waved her arms, motioning for Cassie to start the car. She saw Cassie throw the chips to the floor and pull her seat forward. The engine was going by the time Maggie jumped into the car.

"What in the sam-hell is going on?" Edna asked.

Maggie gasped for breath, wishing once again that she had made it to the gym that week. That was actually a frequent wish on her list. "I heard him on the phone. He's getting ready to go meet her."

"Meet who?" Sunny passed Maggie a bottle of water.

"Charlotte." She pointed to Jeremy's house, where his Toyota 4Runner was backing out of the driveway. "Follow him."

Cassie eased forward, trying to stay far enough back that Jeremy wouldn't notice her car. "Thank goodness that I have the most popular minivan on the planet. There are dozens of cars like mine on the road."

Maggie sank low in the seat. "Still, try to keep a good distance back."

"Yeah, we don't want him to make us." Edna had pulled a ball cap from her giant purse and pulled it on over her silvery hair.

Maggie rolled her eyes. "Make us? Are you serious? What is he gonna make us? A cake?"

Edna rummaged around on the floor of the minivan and came up with another baseball cap. She passed it up to Maggie. "Shut up and put this on. You don't want him to recognize you."

Maggie snatched the hat from Edna's hand and tugged it on her head, pulling her hair through the hole in the back to make a loose ponytail.

Cassie kept her full concentration on the road, keeping an eagle eye on Jeremy's car. "What about me? Find something back there for me. I think my sunhat is in the back from going to the pool earlier this summer."

Piper passed a big floppy black hat up to Sunny, who passed it to Cassie. "Geez, Aunt Cassie. You have tons of crap in this car. Are you preparing for a zombie apocalypse?"

Cassie crushed the big hat onto her head. "No, I'm just a mom. And that's the beauty of driving a minivan, I have everything I could need in here. It's like a giant purse on wheels."

Piper ransacked the floor and various compartments of the van for more disguises and came up with a snorkel and mask, a hockey helmet, and a neon-green pair of sunglasses straight out of the eighties. She held the choices out to Sunny, who took the sunglasses. Piper considered her choices and pulled the hockey helmet over her head.

"He's getting on the highway." Sunny pointed to the on-ramp just as her cell phone rang. She pulled the phone from her purse and put it to her ear. "Hey, Jake."

Maggie listened as Sunny explained what had happened this morning with Jeremy. "Tell him we've been on the highway for about ten minutes. I have a bad feeling we're headed out of town."

Sunny passed on the message, listened a few minutes more, then hung up the phone. "That was Jake. He thinks he knows where Jeremy is going. They were talking earlier this week, and Jeremy told him the big Comic Con is in Denver this weekend and mentioned that he might try to go. I told Jake that it looked like we were headed to Denver, and he said he'll jump in his car and meet us there."

"What the heck is a Comic Con?" Cassie asked.

Edna sighed, like it was such a struggle that she had to explain everything. "It's a big nerd convention they hold every year where everybody dresses like their favorite comic book or super hero, and they bring in a bunch of celebrities from the famous nerd shows, like *Star Trek* and *Star Wars* and *Stargate* and any other show with a 'star' in it."

"How do you know all this, Edna?" Sunny asked.

"It's called the internet. You should try it sometime."

Maggie turned to face the back seat. "That sounds like something Jeremy would totally dig. Is Jake sure that's where he's headed?"

Sunny nodded. "He seemed pretty sure. And by the amount of time we've been on this highway, I'm pretty sure we're headed to Denver."

"Good thing I filled up for the football game this weekend. Oh crud!" Cassie reached for her purse and tossed it in Maggie's lap. "Somebody's gonna need to call Matt and tell him I don't think I'll make it to the kids' game today."

The minivan carrying a hockey player, a movie star, an eighties enthusiast, and a couple of baseball fans pulled into the garage labeled "Comic Con Parking". At least that was how Cassie's van would have looked to an outsider. However, the number of crazy-costumed people that were filing into the convention center told Maggie her band of misfits would fit right in.

They'd followed Jeremy's car into the garage, but had lost sight of it in the maze of the parking structure. Tumbling from the minivan, they all got out and stretched after the hour-long car chase. Once they had been on the highway for half an hour and were fairly certain of their destination, some of the drama went out of the excitement of the chase.

"This way." Piper waved them forward. She had left the hockey helmet in the car, and her blond hair now lay smashed against her head.

Maggie moved forward, so engrossed with watching the costumed participants walk by that she almost ran into Edna, who had come to a dead stop in front of her.

"Edna. Holy crap, I almost ran over you." Maggie sighed. "What are you doing?"

Edna was standing behind an old burgundy-colored car. She had stopped to look at the car and was digging into her purse. "I've seen this car before. It's an old Mercury Marquis, probably from the early eighties. My husband used to have one. Not in this god-awful color, but about the same model."

"That's great that you're enjoying memory lane, but we need to hurry," Sunny said, always the kind one.

At the same time Maggie blurted out, "So what? We gotta go!"

Edna found what she was digging for in her purse and pulled free a pen and a small notebook. "If you'd hold your pea-picking horses, I need to write down the license plate."

"Why? What are you going to do with his license plate number? Track down the owner? Talk about old car memories?" Maggie's impatience came out in her snide tone.

"Yes, I do want to track down the owner. You weren't listening," Edna explained. "I've seen this car before. Because we used to have one, I know they're not very common. Especially not this weird burgundy color. But I saw this one the night we stopped at Jeremy's office. The night Jim was murdered. I'm sure this car was parked in Jeremy's parking lot next to his office."

Maggie's face flamed with heat from shame. This was not the first time her impatience and sarcasm had put her in an embarrassing situation. "Sorry, Edna. I'm just stressed. I shouldn't have been mean."

Edna pushed the notebook back into her purse and started walking. And at a fairly good clip for an elderly woman. She called over her shoulder. "I'm used to it. I still love you. But come on, we've got a nerd to follow."

A teenage boy dressed as a zombie in a Superman costume turned to Edna, obviously overhearing her remark. He smiled at the old lady wearing a baseball cap crookedly on her head and gave her a thumbs-up sign. "Right on."

The book club stepped out of the garage into the blinding sun and came to a dead stop. Not as dead as the zombie Superman, but they stopped nonetheless. The only one not squinting against the bright sun was Sunny, who still wore the neon-green sunglasses.

"Holy geek-squad. That is a lot of nerds." Piper held her arm up to block the sun.

A huge banner stating "Welcome to Comic Con" hung above the convention center's main doors. From the doors, a line of every imaginable costumed comic book character snaked around the building for a good city block.

The women walked to the back of the line, passing Jedi warriors, Storm Troopers, a couple of Batmans, at least three Spider-Mans, and several Spocks. It seemed every woman they passed was barely wearing some form of a slutty character's outfit. Maggie didn't think *that* many female characters sported so much cleavage.

Cassie groaned. They'd finally made it to the back of the line. "We're gonna be in this line forever."

"Yeah, and I haven't seen Jeremy in the last ten minutes." Piper craned her neck to look up the rows of people standing in front of them.

"I tried to watch as we walked past the line and I never saw him," Maggie said.

"I tried to watch too, but I kept getting distracted, looking at all the costumes." Edna pointed toward the front of the line. "Did you see that big guy up there dressed as Chewbacca? That looked like real fur."

"Like real fur? From what? A Wookie?" A stab of pain hit her in the heart at the reminder of the big dog that had recently captured Jeremy's heart. A heart she felt she had a place in. At least up until a few hours ago. Maggie shook her head and focused back on Edna. "And quit pointing."

Edna shrugged. "Hey, you wouldn't put on a Chewbacca costume and not expect a few people to point at you."

"That's a true statement," Sunny said, then reached for her pocket as her cell phone rang. She pulled it free and held it to her ear. "Hey, Jake." She listened for a few seconds, then looked around and nodded. "I see it. We'll meet you over there."

She snapped the phone shut and pulled the women out of line and toward a door marked "Staff Only— West Entrance."

"That was Jake. He's already inside. He's gonna let us in."

Speak of the gorgeous devil, the staff entrance door opened and Jake stood there, grinning like a kid in a candy store. "This place is so cool. Have you seen all these costumes?"

Sunny pushed up on her toes, planting a kiss on Jake's cheek. "Yes, honey. We have seen a few costumes."

Each of the women said hi to Jake as they walked past him and into the dimly lit area beyond the door. It looked to be a storage area of some sort, with boxes and conference-type equipment stacked on the floor.

Jake stopped Maggie as she came through the door, pulling her into a tight hug and speaking into her ear. "I know this looks bad, but don't give up on him. I really believe Jeremy is a good guy. There's going to be a reasonable explanation to this."

Maggie squeezed him back, fighting against the pin prick of tears that his words brought to her eyes. She wanted to believe what Jake was saying. She wanted to believe that this was all some strange set of coincidences. That Jeremy hadn't lied and that he hadn't stayed overnight in a motel with the cleavage-laden blond programmer. Maybe they were just working. She wanted to believe him, but her prior experience with men told her otherwise. "Thanks, Jake. I hope you're right."

The group gathered around Jake and he passed them each a lanyard with a clear pouch attached to it and what looked like a hotel key card encased in the pouch. "Here, put these on. They're your passes to get into the convention. Everyone is wearing one."

Sunny pulled the lanyard over her head. "How did you get these?"

"It's all about knowing a guy." Jake gave her one of his killer grins. "And I know a guy that's up here working security for the convention. Bobby and I worked together on a case several years back. I called him as I was driving up. He let me in and had VIP passes waiting for all of us. These will get you into any area of the Con."

"Good job," Maggie said. "But have you seen Jeremy?"

Jake nodded. "I saw him across the convention floor about ten minutes ago, but he was too far away to get to. I did see his costume, though."

"What? He's in a costume?" Maggie couldn't believe that he just happened to have a costume all prepared in the back of his car. "That must have been what he was carrying in the duffel bag. But why would he have that in his car?"

"I told you that he talked to me about his plans to come up to this." Jake said. "But with Jim's death, he wasn't sure if he should come."

Anger flared in Maggie's gut. He had told Jake about his plans, but not her. What else was he keeping from her? "I guess a call from his 'girlfriend' must have convinced him."

Sunny laid a comforting hand on Maggie's arm. "Don't jump to any conclusions. We haven't heard Jeremy's side of the story yet."

Maggie wouldn't jump to any conclusions, but she might jump on a certain blond bimbo's head and then do a pile-driver with an elbow to her side. "All right, so what's our plan? How are we going to find Jeremy?"

"That may be a problem," Jake explained. "His costume is some Jedi Knight thing. I think it's Obi-Wan Kenobi's."

"Why is that a problem?" Piper asked. "Even I could recognize that."

"Because there are only about a hundred and fifty other Jedi Knight costumes out there. Wait until you step on the convention floor. It's madness." Jake leaned back and looked the group over, obviously surveying their disguises. "And you all are gonna stick out like crazy. We need some costumes to blend in."

Jake led them through the maze of behind-the-scenes equipment and stopped at the back of a large booth surrounded by thick royal-purple curtains. He pulled the curtain back, and they stepped into a large vendor booth with rows of hangered costumes and props lining the curtained walls.

A slim, dark-haired woman in her mid-forties wearing a skin-tight black cat suit with shiny yellow boots, a yellow utility belt, and a yellow Batman symbol on her chest, approached them from the front of the booth. "You must be Jake." Her voice was smooth as velvet, and she smiled warmly at the book club members. "And these are your friends. Bobby told me you might be stopping by. I'm Allegra, and I'll be happy to help any way I can."

"Thanks, Allegra." Jake smiled at her, then gestured to the women surrounding him. "This is Sunny, Maggie, Cassie, Edna, and Piper. We all need costumes that will allow us to blend in, but disguise who we are. And we need them quickly."

Allegra stepped back and looked each of them up and down. She moved her mouth from side to side, as if this helped her think or determine their sizes. "Okay, I think I've got it. Look around to see if you see anything special you love, otherwise I'll be back in a minute with some ideas." She disappeared up one of the rows of clothing.

The group spread out, marveling at the choices. Maggie looked around in dismay at the walls of props. "I hate dressing up. I don't even like Halloween. Can't I just wear this ball cap?"

Cassie, who was the best shopper of the bunch, was already rifling through the hangers. "Oh, stop it. Jeremy could pick you out of a crowd in a second. For once, just go with the flow." She held up a green ninja suit. "How about this one? You could wear a ninja hood over your hair."

Maggie gave her one of her looks. "Put that back." Pulling out one of the price tags, she almost choked. She looked up at Jake. "We can't afford six of these costumes. These are ridiculously expensive."

Jake held up a shiny credit card. "Oh yes, we can. Jeremy's buying. He gave me a corporate card and told me to use it for whatever will help the investigation. If this helps, then great, money well spent. If we find out he's a lying cheat, which I don't think he is, then it will serve him right to have to pay for these."

Although a tad skewed, Maggie liked his logic. She decided it wouldn't hurt to dress up. A little. If it helped them to fit in.

Allegra appeared, her arms laden with colored fabrics and plastic bags of props. She pointed to the wall, which was cordoned off with tiny curtained dressing rooms. "I tried to find ones that had a mask or something to cover your faces." She handed them each a costume.

Piper and Edna must have found something they liked, because they were already tucked behind two of the curtained rooms.

Handing one of the bags to Cassie, Allegra winked. "I can tell this outfit is going to be perfect for you. And it will show off your best features."

Cassie was constantly talking about going on a diet and the extra weight she had put on since having the kids. Maggie thought she looked great and carried the little extra "mom" weight with the confidence of a woman who was happily married and knew she was loved and adored by a man waiting for her at home.

"I thought you might enjoy being Batgirl." Allegra passed a bagged costume to Sunny.

Sunny looked at the bag and at Allegra's skin-tight cat suit with dismay. "There is no way that I am getting my curves into a little suit like that."

Allegra laughed. "Don't worry. This costume is a little different style. I think you'll love it."

Jake looked down at the gray and black costume Allegra had handed him and a huge grin lit up his face. He grabbed Sunny by the waist and pulled her into the dressing room with him. "Come on, Sunny. We can share this one and you can help me with the zipper."

Maggie took the costume and plastic bag of props from Allegra and stepped behind a curtain. She could hear Sunny giggling from behind the curtained wall of her fitting room. "No hanky-panky in there. Just get dressed. We have work to do."

"Don't be such a buzz-kill." Edna's voice drifted up from another dressing room. "There's always time for a little hanky-panky."

Maggie shook her head and put on the outfit Allegra had chosen for her. She had to smile a little. The shop owner couldn't have picked a better costume for the closet gamer that she was. Maggie looked at herself in the mirror.

She wore a black tank top tucked into a slim pair of black shorts. Two gun holsters hung down from the edges of the shorts and the straps wrapped around her upper thighs. Tall military boots with black socks completed the outfit. She pulled her hair into a long ponytail at the back of her head, and her transformation was complete. She was a dead ringer for *Tomb Raider's* Lara Croft.

She stepped from the curtained room and laughed in delight as Cassie stood in front of her in a Wonder Woman costume. She wore tall shiny red boots, and her full hips were covered by a blue skirt covered in white stars. Gold cuffs enclosed each of her wrists, and a matching gold tiara was stuck in the long black wig that covered Cassie's blond hair. A red corset top pushed Cassie's "best features" up, and a red cape was tied at her neck. Cassie's face gleamed with a bit of a naughty smile as she twirled in front of her friend. "What do you think?"

"It's perfect." Sunny stepped from the dressing room wearing a short black neoprene dress. The same yellow Batman symbol and utility belt that Allegra wore adorned Sunny's dress, but the short skirt was more fitting to Sunny's curves. She also had a black cape tied around her neck and a black bat-shaped mask covered her face. Shiny yellow high-heeled boots made Sunny two inches taller.

Maggie laughed. "You guys look great. Cassie, I wouldn't even recognize you in that black wig. And Sunny, I love the Batgirl outfit. Now all you need is the Dark Knight to go with it."

"She already has him." A deep, throaty voice spoke from the dressing room, and Jake stepped out in a full Batman costume, complete with a rubberized black hood covering his head and eyes. Every muscle in Jake's hard body was outlined in a light gray body suit. He wore a black utility belt over black Speedo-style trunks. Tall black boots encased his calves. Jake wore a goofy grin, and he lost the deep Batman voice in favor of one reminiscent of his junior high years. "Isn't this the coolest?"

Maggie blinked, not quite sure what to say. All she could think was that Sunny was one lucky woman.

"Holy hotness, Batman!" Leave it to Edna. She always had something to say.

Maggie turned to look at Edna at the same time that Piper pulled back the curtain and stepped from the dressing room. "What the heck? You've got to be kidding me."

Cassie and Sunny broke into laughter as they regarded their fellow book club members.

Edna and Piper *both* wore the same costume of a Catholic school girl.

However, Piper's short kilted skirt fit perfectly on her petite teenage frame. She wore white knee socks with short lace-up boots. She had tied the white button-up in a knot at her waist, a thin band of her flat stomach visible below the shirt. To complete her ensemble, she wore a wig of neon blue hair tied into high ponytails on either side of her head.

One of Edna's knee socks was bunched around her ankle above her thick-soled orthopedic old-lady shoes. Her white shirt was buttoned to her neck, and she wore a striped necktie. The skirt of her outfit hung low above her wrinkled bony knees.

Piper examined Edna's outfit and gave a sigh of exasperation. "Edna, you are one crazy old lady."

Edna smiled mischievously. "You got that right."

Maggie finally found her voice. "What the heck are you two supposed to be?"

Piper pointed at Edna. "I don't know for sure what she's supposed to be, but I am a character from *Sailor Moon*. It's anime. Like animated Japanese cartoons. I just need a sword."

Allegra passed Piper a plastic sword and holster from the props behind her. "This should work. And I have something for you too, Miss Edna. I'll be right back." She disappeared around the clothes rack.

"This is great." Piper buckled the holster across her chest.

"Where's my sword?" Edna asked. "I think I could do some serious swash-buckling."

Piper rolled her eyes. "We're not pirates, Edna."

Allegra emerged from the clothes rack with a long black robe in her hands. "Here, this will work perfectly. Put this on over your outfit, pull the hood up, and you will totally pass for Hermione Granger."

Jake took the robe from her and held it out for Edna to slide her arms into. Once she had it on, the Hogwarts insignia was visible on the right breast pocket.

Edna pulled the hood over her hair. "Hey, this isn't bad. And I'm so short, I could totally pass for a teenager."

Not one person had the guts to argue with her.

Allegra handed Maggie a black ball cap and a pair of mirrored Aviator sunglasses. "I brought these for you. They're Lara's style, and may help to mask your identity."

"Good thinking." Maggie pulled the cap and glasses on. "Okay. I think we're ready. Let's go find Jeremy."

Piper held out her hand. "I was thinking that we don't want to be lugging all of our regular clothes around. Aunt Cassie, if you give me your keys, I'll take everybody's stuff out to the car."

Cassie nodded. "Good idea. I'll come with you, then we can meet up with everyone inside the main convention area."

Maggie handed Cassie her purse and stack of clothes. "Call my cell when you come back in, and I'll tell you where we are." She smacked her forehead with her hand. "Never mind. I have no phone. Mine took a face-plant into a toilet. Call Sunny's phone."

Once Jake handed Allegra the credit card, she made short work of ringing up their costumes. Maggie saw the receipt she passed back to him and cringed at the total. Oh well. According to Jake, Jeremy could afford it.

Allegra gave them some bags to put all their clothes in, and Piper and Cassie headed out the back curtains. Batman, Batgirl, Lara Croft, and a wrinkly Hermione moved to the front of the booth to enter the main convention floor.

The noise hit them first and Maggie's senses were overloaded with the sound of excited voices, splashes of colored costumes, rock music playing in the background, and a subtle hint of body odor. The room was crowded and warm. Apparently not everyone washed their costumes in between conventions.

Maggie was overwhelmed with the sheer number of people packed into one room. Vendor booths lined the walls, with rows of booths running down the center creating a maze of comic-book-character-filled rows. Signs directed participants to the various entertainment areas of the conference, citing where to find lectures, autograph signings, and star appearances. The stars were toward the back, and long lines of costumed characters snaked down the rows, making passage through those areas even more clogged and congested. "Where do we start?"

Jake stood on a chair and scanned the crowded room. "Look for a guy wearing a Jedi Knight costume with the hood up."

Edna stood on her tip-toes, but the crowd engulfed her small frame. "I can't see a durn thing. Except a bunch of cleavage walking by. Cover those things up! They're called privates for a reason!"

Maggie surveyed the room, ignoring Edna, who frequently dispensed advice to innocent bystanders. Once, in the mall, she told the gal at the cosmetics counter that she was wearing too much makeup. Catching sight of a brown hood, Maggie pointed. "I see one."

Sunny had climbed onto the chair next to Jake and pointed in the opposite direction of Maggie. "I see one too. He's headed to the lectures."

Jake groaned. "I see one, too. In fact, now that I'm looking, I see about fifty of them. This is going to be like looking for a needle in a haystack."

"Or a light saber in a nerd field." Edna jabbed Maggie in the ribs. "Come on, that was kind of funny."

Maggie continued to ignore her friend and looked up Jake. "What should we do? Split up?"

Jake stepped off the chair and held out his hand to help Sunny down. "I guess we're gonna have to. Sunny and I will head to the lectures. You and Edna check the gaming area. Sunny can text Cass, and when she and Piper come back in, they can go over to the autograph signings. We know Jeremy is tall, so that should help eliminate some of the Jedis. Whoever spots him first, text or call, then we'll each head that way."

Before Maggie could ask to trade tracking partners, Edna pulled on her arm.

"I think I see one," Edna said, then disappeared into the throng of people, leaving Maggie no choice but to follow her.

Up ahead, Maggie could see a tall guy wearing a brown hood. Edna was in hot pursuit, pushing people aside to get to the Jedi Knight. Maggie followed in her wake, and she couldn't help but smile as she watched Edna's maneuvers for clearing a crowd. The little old lady poked, prodded, and pinched at whoever stood in her way. By the look of surprise on a *Star Trek* captain's face, Maggie was pretty sure Edna had goosed him as she squeezed by.

The Jedi Knight had stopped at a cardboard box of comic books in front of a booth. Maggie could see

Edna creeping up on him. Before Maggie could stop her, she watched Edna stick a foot out and stand on the tail of the Jedi's cape. The knight took a step forward and his head jerked back and the hood fell off, revealing a very surprised freckled teenager with bright orange hair. So *not* Jeremy.

Before the red-haired Jedi could spot his cape-treader, Edna disappeared into the crowd, popping up at Maggie's elbow. "That wasn't him. Can you spot another one?"

Maggie had to hand it to her. Her geriatric pal had skills. "I can see that. Maybe try for a little more distance with the next one. What if he'd spotted you?"

Edna huffed. "Then all he would have seen was a teenage girl in a Hogwarts cape."

"You wish." Maggie scanned the heads of the crowd. "Oh, I see another one. Head left to the gaming area."

With the determination of a terrier, Edna plunged back into the crowd. Maggie tailed her, trying to keep an eye on the brown-hooded Jedi they were tracking. They stepped into the row of gaming booths then Maggie lost sight of him.

She did notice a booth for SkyVision though. Jeremy had told her that company was his main competitor. Maggie pulled on Edna's sleeve. "This booth is Jeremy's company's main competition. Let's go check it out."

Edna nodded, and they moved into the vendor area. The booth for SkyVision was large, taking up two booth rental spots. It was decorated to look like a high-end living room with a sofa set in the middle, facing a wall of flat-screen televisions. Each screen showed a different game being played, the table in front of the sofa scattered with an array of game controllers.

A young blond guy, somewhere in his mid-twenties, approached them. He was wearing a Captain America suit, complete with bright blue tights and the Captain America symbol emblazoned on his well-muscled chest. He wore the outfit with the confidence of a well-built guy and Maggie could feel the conceit wafting off of him as he strode toward them.

"Can I help you, ladies? Are you looking for the autograph stations?"

Maggie gestured to the controllers. "Can anyone use these?"

Barely hiding his sneer, Captain America dipped his head at Maggie. "Have *you* ever played a video game before?"

Maggie wanted to smack the snide look right off of his stupid twenty-something face. She had no use for this arrogant little snob of a kid who had probably just crawled out of college. "Not much. I've just been playing *World of Warcraft* for the past two years, and I'm a level ninety Draenei with Tier 13 PVP Gladiator Gear."

Captain America's sneer of conceit changed to one of astonishment. "I stand corrected. Respectfully so." He gestured to Edna, who still had the Hogwarts robe pulled over her face. "And does your daughter play as well?"

Edna pushed back her hood, displaying her springy gray curls. "I'm not her daughter, and I don't know what the hell she just said. She could have just told you she's the Queen of England, for all I know. I don't waste my time with this mind-numbing baloney. I prefer to feed my brain with actual knowledge. Through these little known things called books. Ever heard of them?"

Maggie pushed Edna behind her, rolling her eyes. "She's my grandmother. You know, kinda kooky. Why don't you tell me something new and exciting that SkyVision is doing?"

His face lit up, and he launched into a lengthy speech about a new gaming system that his company was working on. Maggie had worked with enough men to know that all you had to do to get them talking was ask about something they were interested in and had a vague knowledge about and they could talk for hours. She was glad this was the case with Captain America and didn't have to resort to false compliments like "Wow, what a big controller you have." *Gag.*

He introduced himself as Skyler Humphries and explained that SkyVision was his company. He went on to tell her how this new system was a design that he had been working on for years.

What? Since you were twelve? How could he own his own company already? And every detail he was telling her about this system sounded exactly like the program that Jeremy's company had been working on. And the only way he could have known about it was if this punk had been the one to pay off Jim to get the information.

She waited for him to take a breath so she could nonchalantly throw out a question. "That sounds really interesting. But isn't Rogers' Realms working on something similar?"

"What? What do know about Rogers' Realms?" The question obviously flustered Skyler. "This is nothing like what they have. And if they do, then they must have stolen it from us."

Maggie held in her scoff. Yeah, right. She couldn't see Jeremy stealing anything from this guy. Besides, Jeremy had too much integrity to steal from someone else.

Hmmm. That thought hit her right in the chest. She didn't think Jeremy would steal company secrets, but she believed him capable of cheating on her and possibly committing murder?

Maybe this was all stupid. She should just sit down with Jeremy and talk this out. Find out his explanation for lying about being with Charlotte in a motel room. Wait, oh yeah. She couldn't talk to him because he wasn't answering his phone. He was running around a giant Nerd-a-thon dressed as a fictitious crime fighter.

Maggie stared directly at Skyler, giving him her best lawyer's glare. "How do we know that you didn't steal it from them?"

"What? Why would I?" He took a step back. Maggie could smell the guilt on him, as strong as the odor of tuna fish to a cat.

Before he could say more, the back curtain of the booth opened, and a woman dressed as Poison Ivy emerged from between the curtain folds. "Skyler, I can't find that box with the—oh sorry, I didn't realize you had company." She looked at Maggie, as if she were trying to place how she knew her.

The woman wore a very short, glittery, bright green dress adorned with leaves, and had a grapevine wreath wrapped around her arms and upper thighs. She wore shiny four-inch green heels and a bright red wig. The red hair cascaded in thick waves around her shoulders, and Maggie knew it was a wig, because no one's hair was naturally that color.

And because she knew the color of that woman's hair was actually blond. No amount of glittery makeup or fake hair could disguise the milky white globes of cleavage popping out of the slutty green dress and the sway of the hips that walked toward them. How fitting that Charlotte Foster would dress as Poison Ivy, a villain instead of a hero.

Edna must have recognized her as well because Maggie felt her pulling her hood back on and tugging her into the crowd.

Maggie ducked her head, pulling the ball cap lower over her mirrored sunglasses. "I'll be back later to hear more about this." Then she turned and disappeared into the crowd behind Hermione Granger in orthopedic shoes.

Two hours and twelve incorrect Jedi Knights later, Maggie and Edna stood in the front of the concession booth, guzzling down Diet Coke like it was water.

Maggie had used Edna's phone to text the rest of the group to meet in the food area, thinking they could all benefit from a cold drink and some nourishment. The drink was easy, but finding actual nourishment was going to be a little harder. The food vendors were limited and served cafeteria-style fare. They could get a hamburger or chicken fingers, but a salad would be a stretch.

Cassie and Piper were the first to arrive. Piper bounced along with excitement, but Cassie looked ready to drop. She plucked the cup right from Maggie's hand and took a big swallow.

"Thanks. I needed that." She said the words like Maggie had just given her a shot of whiskey instead of a sip of soda, but everyone had their own vice.

"Any luck?" Maggie asked.

Piper shook her head. "Nah—we followed seven Jedis, but none of them turned out to be Jeremy."

"But we did see one extremely hairy, heavy guy wearing the same Wonder Woman outfit that I have on. So there was that to be excited about." Cassie dug in her pocket and pulled out some wadded bills. "Piper, honey, run over there and get us some pop and some French fries. And some chicken fingers."

"And some nachos," Edna called out to Piper's retreating back. She shrugged at her friends. "Hey, a girl's gotta eat."

Cassie nodded. "Yeah, all this surveillance is making me hungry."

Batman and Batgirl came around the corner. Maggie hoped they had better news. "Any luck?" she asked again.

Jake sighed. "No luck. I was pretty sure we had him a couple times, but one guy turned out to be a really tall woman, and we lost the other one in the crowd."

Sunny took Maggie's cup and took a drink. "Did you see that line of people waiting to get autographs? The one time we were sure it was him, we tried to catch up with him and got stuck in that throng of people. Every time we tried to squeeze through, people thought we were trying to cut in line and pushed us back."

Maggie took her cup back. Evidently she should have bought a bigger drink. "We never found him either. But we did see Charlotte."

"You did?" Sunny said. "Did she see you?"

"Yeah, but I don't think she recognized me. She looked at me like she thought she should know me, but I never saw a light of recognition go off in her slutty/cheater eyes."

"You talking about Charlotte?" Piper returned with enough food to feed an army, or at least a small battalion, of weary super heroes. She set the snacks on an empty table and they all pulled out chairs and sat down. "Edna texted me what she was wearing, and I'm pretty sure we saw her. One of our Jedis was talking to a busty redhead in a sparkly green dress, but we couldn't get close enough to see if it was Jeremy, then we lost them. Geez, did anyone try to get through that line of people waiting for autographs?"

"I know, right? I was just saying that." Sunny laughed and pulled a nacho from Edna's tray. She hesitated before putting the chip in her mouth and a funny look crossed her face.

Maggie was sure she was thinking back to earlier this summer when she dumped a tray of nachos down the back of a couple of unsuspecting baseball fans on a date that ended horribly wrong. She reached out and took her friend's hand. "You okay, Sunny?"

Sunny squeezed her hand and gave her that smile that you give your closest friends who can almost always guess what you're thinking about. "Of course. It just brought back the memories for a second of all those crazy dates earlier this summer."

Maggie motioned to the man in gray tights wearing a Batman hood. "It all worked out in the end."

Sunny smiled, a huge grin crossing her face and lighting up her eyes. "Yes, it did." She looked Maggie in the eye. "And it's going to work out for you too. You'll see."

Maggie rolled her eyes. Why couldn't she bottle some of her friend's optimism and guzzle down a few cups? She wished she could just simply believe in

Jeremy and his innocence. In both the false alibi and the accusation of murder. Because she had believed before, believed in true love, and that if you married someone, you would stay with them forever, and not run off with a waitress from Hooters. She knew how that turned out.

The group of friends finished off the snacks, and Cassie threw the trays into the garbage.

Maggie looked expectantly at Jake. "What's our next move?"

Jake used a black-gloved hand to rub his chin in thought. "Maybe we should just flush him out. We could find someone here who could send him an anonymous text and tell him to meet them at the food vendor area."

Edna bobbed her head up and down. "Yeah. Then we could hide and follow him after he shows up. I like it."

Piper turned to a table of three teenage boys wearing *Star Wars* bounty hunter outfits. "Hey, can I borrow one of your phones for a sec? My friend is ignoring me, and I want to see if I send her a text from a different phone if she'll answer."

One of the boys reached into the folds of his bounty hunter robes and extracted a cell phone. "Is your friend hot? Maybe I can keep her number in my phone, and I can text her later."

Piper took the phone and copied Jeremy's number onto the keypad from Edna's contacts. She typed a quick message, pushed send, then passed the phone back to the boys. "You can try. But she's kind of a B. She probably won't answer."

Piper turned back to the table and lowered her voice. "Okay, I wrote 'for info about Jim's death, meet me by the food court, in front of the light saber display'. How's that?"

Jake smiled at her. "Perfect. Now we better get out of here in case he's close."

The group scattered in all directions, taking up hiding places around the crowded food court. Maggie laughed at Edna, who was nonchalantly holding a conversation with a Princess Leia in a gold bikini holding a Jabba the Hutt on a chain.

Her laughter died on her lips as she saw a tall Jedi Knight come around the corner and stride to the little vendor cart full of light sabers. Everything in her wanted to call off this stupid charade and just go to him and talk it out.

Before she could take a step forward, a flash of glittery green caught her eye. She stepped back into the folds of a curtained booth, watching as Charlotte strode forward, calling out Jeremy's name. Maggie's heart broke just a little as she saw Charlotte approach him and throw her arms around his neck.

To Jeremy's credit, he reached back and pulled her arms free. He moved back slightly, as if to put some distance between them. But evidently Charlotte was new to the term *personal space* and pushed her giant breasts forward.

Jeremy had his head tipped down, and they were deep in conversation. Maggie moved along the curtained booth, trying to get closer. She smiled as she saw Piper fall in line with a group of teenagers, then stop to look at a box of comic books in a booth about six feet from Jeremy. With her blue-haired pigtails, she looked like any other teenaged girl at the convention.

Maggie moved a little closer, stepping in front of a booth filled with *Star Trek* paraphernalia. She saw Charlotte nod at Jeremy and smiled a little when she saw Jeremy take a step back as Charlotte moved to hug him again.

Maybe he really wasn't messing around with her. Maybe Charlotte lied about being with him. But the motel clerk had backed up her story. Maggie felt so confused. Maybe they were having an affair, and Jeremy just didn't want her hugging him in public so no one would suspect them.

Maggie turned to a display of telecommunicators and wished Scotty could just beam her up right now. She heard the click of Charlotte's heels pass behind her and move down the hall. What now? Should she confront Jeremy? Did they go through this entire charade just to witness that miniscule exchange with Charlotte? That none of them could even hear. Except maybe Piper. Hopefully she picked up some snippets of their conversation.

"Look who's headed this way."

Maggie jumped as Edna appeared next to her elbow. Maybe Edna should have worn that ninja costume. With those thick-soled shoes, she could sneak up on anyone. Maggie started to turn but Edna batted at her arm.

"Don't look over there. You don't want to be too obvious." Edna kept her voice low, talking out of the side of her mouth. "I just wonder what Captain America is so excited to talk to our Jedi about."

Maggie moved deeper into the booth and swept her hand over a stack of Captain Kirk uniform shirts. Turning her head, she saw Skyler approach Jeremy, and he did not look happy. She watched Jeremy's back stiffen so he stood an inch taller, possibly trying to intimidate the smaller and younger man.

Yeah, right. Jeremy was about as intimidating as Clark Kent. Maggie only prayed that he turned out to be Superman underneath and not Lex Luthor.

This time, they didn't have to get closer to hear the conversation. The way they started yelling, everyone around them heard it.

Jeremy's raised voice carried to Maggie and Edna. "You're trying to tell me you just came up with this new system, that's identical to mine, and just happened to be launching the same week as my company's? That's bull."

Captain America shouted back: "You're not the only one around here who can invent new code."

"You didn't invent anything except more stupidity. There is no way that you created the exact same gaming system that we did in the same few months."

"What are you accusing me of?"

"You've been trying to convince me how brilliant you are. Why don't you figure it out?"

Good one, Jeremy. Maggie tried to act engrossed in the comic books in the box in front of her, but she was thrilled to hear Jeremy putting that little conceited jerk in his place.

Skyler puffed up his Captain America-clad chest and took a step closer to Jeremy. "What I've figured out is that when people don't agree you with you at your company, they end up dead."

That comment must have been too much for Jeremy. Without a moment's hesitation, his right arm came up and he punched Skyler right in his smug, cocky little face.

Skyler howled in pain, very un-Avenger like, and reached for his nose, which was now dripping blood on his shiny blue bodysuit. "You punched me," he said, his voice full of disbelief.

Jeremy leaned forward, his voice low, but full of force. "Don't you ever talk about Jim like that again. He was a good man, and now he's gone. And if you *ever* accuse me of hurting my employees again, I will sue you for slander so fast that your head will spin."

Skyler pulled his hand back and looked at his bloody palm. The expression on his face changed from one of disbelief to a look of rage. He slammed into Jeremy, tackling him to the ground and throwing punches at his chest and face.

Out of nowhere, a flash of black and gray appeared, and Batman was there, lifting Skyler from Jeremy's body. Batman easily held the smaller Captain America in a one-armed choke hold while he reached down to offer a hand to the Jedi Knight.

Jeremy waved his hand away and stood on his own, straightening his clothes and the costumes cloak. He nodded at the caped crusader. "Thanks, Batman."

The Batman patted Jeremy on the shoulder. "You all right, man?"

Maggie heard Jake's reply and saw Jeremy's flash of recognition at his friend's voice. A strange look crossed his face. She couldn't tell if he was just surprised and confused that Jake was there and wearing a Batman costume, or if it was something more.

Could he be nervous about Jake showing up at the Comic Con? Worried that he may have seen him with Charlotte or maybe just bothered that Jake saved him in a fight? There were too many questions and not enough answers. It was time to talk to Jeremy.

A small crowd had gathered around the men, some cheering Batman on, thinking this was part of the con's entertainment.

Maggie saw Jake talking into Skyler's ear, and she could tell by their faces that it was not a pleasant conversation. Maggie almost smiled, as she could hear that Jake was using the deep-throated Batman voice to tell Skyler he needed to walk away.

Jake released the smaller man, and Skyler gave Jeremy a glare filled with hate. "This isn't over, Rogers." He stomped off in the direction of the autograph signings.

Jeremy approached Jake, shaking his hand and thanking him for the help. A couple of teenagers in the crowd snapped pictures. "What are you doing here, Jake?" he asked.

"The more important question is, what are you doing here? Meeting up with your girlfriend?" Edna had appeared at Jeremy's elbow and he looked down at the person in the Hogwarts cape in confusion. Edna pushed back her hood with a grand "ta-da" gesture, as if she had just unveiled the magician behind the trick.

"Edna, what are you doing here? And why are you dressed like that?" Jeremy looked baffled and mildly amused as he searched the crowd behind her. "Is my grandma here too? You guys are a hoot."

"Mabel's not here. I didn't want to bring her along to see this. But I did bring a few other ladies that are pretty interested in what kind of shenanigans you're getting into up here. " Edna waved the others in, and they each stepped forward from their hiding places.

Wonder Woman and Batgirl had been searching through a box of comics in one of the stalls, and Piper had been trying out light sabers. Jeremy's face lit with surprise and laughter as he took in their costumes and then recognized each one. "You guys look awesome. But what are you doing here?" He scanned the surrounding booths. "And where's Maggie?"

She stepped out from behind the curtain of the *Star Wars* booth, pulling her sunglasses from her face. "I'm here."

The tone of her voice had Jeremy's look of excitement fall from his face, and suspicion took its place. "What's going on? Why are you all in costumes? Are you spying on me?"

Edna raised her hand. "Ding! Ding! Ding! Give that man a prize! Good deduction, Sherlock."

Jeremy looked to Maggie, waiting for her to answer.

She nodded. "Yeah, we followed you up here. I wanted to see—" Emotion choked her voice and she swallowed back the tears threatening to fall. She did not want to cry in front of all these people. "I wanted to see why you were meeting Charlotte."

Jeremy looked confused. "Charlotte? What does she have to do with anything? And who said I was meeting her?"

Sunny moved to Maggie, putting a protective hand on her friend's arm. "You can drop the act, Jeremy. We know about you and Charlotte. About the affair."

"Affair? What are you talking about?" He took a step toward Maggie. "How could you think that? I'm not having an affair with her. Or with anyone. Where would you get such an idea?"

"From the police." Edna pointed a finger at him. "They told us that your alibi was as false as a set of dentures. That you were really spending the night in a motel with Miss Green-Glitter Hussy-Pants."

"Spending the night in a motel? With Charlotte? That's insane." Jeremy turned to Jake. "Where would they get such a ridiculous notion?"

Jake pulled the Batman mask from his head, his face holding a serious look. "From Charlotte herself. She went to the police and told them you couldn't have killed Jim because you were in a motel that night. With her."

Jeremy looked genuinely shocked. Either he was actually surprised by this news or he was a damn good actor. Maggie wasn't sure which. "Why would she make up something like that?"

Jeremy shook his head, seeming to be honestly dismayed. "I have no idea. Maybe to protect me. But I can assure you that it's not true. I've never been to a motel with her. I've never been with her at all. I was home that night. Alone."

"Prove it," Piper said. "Call her right now and get her to come back here. We all saw you talking to her a few minutes ago. Tell her to come back and get her to admit she lied."

Jeremy pulled out his phone and pushed her contact info. "Fine. That's a great idea. I have some questions for her too." He growled in frustration. "It went to voicemail."

"That's convenient," Edna muttered.

Jeremy rolled his eyes and left a voice message. "Hey, Charlotte, it's Jeremy. I'm hoping you're still at the con. I wanted to talk to you again. Call me back or text me where you are, and I'll come meet you." He ended the call and put the phone back into his pocket. "What now?"

Jake pulled his mask back on. "I say we go find her. We all saw her, and she stands out in that green get-up she's got on. Let's see if we can track her down and get her to tell us why she lied."

"Good idea." Jeremy reached for Maggie's hand. "Will you stay with me?"

Maggie's throat constricted on those five simple words and the meaning they held. Her eyes filled with tears again, and she looked away so Jeremy wouldn't see her crying. She knew he was only asking if she would stay with him right now and help her to search for Charlotte, but the weight of his words and the question it posed sat heavily on her heart.

Would she stay with him? Could she? She needed some answers. She had to find out the truth about Jeremy and Charlotte and who was lying. But could her heart take being broken again? Could she take a chance on Jeremy? She wanted so much to believe in him. She squeezed Jeremy's hand and looked up into his eyes. "Yes, I'll stay with you."

Before they could take a step, a flash of red caught Maggie's eye, and she pulled back on Jeremy's hand.

She pointed across the food court area to a man wearing a red Superman cape and a blue bodysuit.

What was up with all these men wearing bodysuits? And where did they even find them? This man did not have the muscular body of Jake to fill out the suit, so it hung loosely on his thin frame. He was looking directly at them, then he turned and strode off, disappearing into the crowd of people heading into the main convention hall.

Maggie looked to Jeremy for confirmation. "Wasn't that Leonard? The guy who works in your office?"

"I don't get it. Where could she have gone?" Jeremy checked his phone one more time before unlocking the car door and holding it open for Maggie. "And why isn't she responding to my texts or phone calls?"

They had searched the conference for an hour and a half before giving up. They hadn't seen a speck of glittering green dress or poofy red hair. They had seen plenty of Superman costumes, but no sign of Leonard again. It was as if they had vanished into thin air.

Both Charlotte and Leonard could have been avoiding them. Or, on the less mysterious side, they had most likely just had enough of the convention and went home.

Which was what the Page Turners and crew had elected to do. Sunny and Edna decided to ride back to Pleasant Valley with Jake. They offered to walk Cassie and Piper back to the minivan.

Maggie had thought it was a good idea to ride back with Jeremy, but as she climbed in the front seat of the car, she was rethinking her decision. What would they talk about in the car for an hour? If he did cheat on her or if he didn't? If he did kill his employee or if he didn't?

If he was a murderer, she should probably be afraid of him. But as he climbed into the car, his face drawn with worry and adjusting his Jedi cape behind him, all she felt was love…or a really intense like. Geez. Was she really ready to admit that she was falling in love with this guy? Even after hearing he was supposedly shacked up in a motel with Miss Poison Ivy Charlotte?

Maybe that was what this really was—Charlotte spreading her poison, and like a branch of ivy, it was winding its way around her, trying to choke out her feelings for Jeremy.

She jumped as Jeremy laid a hand on her bare leg. "You okay, Mags?" He looked like he was more concerned for her than he was about himself.

All she wanted was for him to wrap his long arms around her and tell her this whole thing was a big mistake. She just wanted to look in his eyes and see the truth and tell him that she believed him. But she had believed Chad too. Believed him every time he said he had a business meeting or had to meet a client for drinks. She had believed every lying word out of his mouth, right up until the day he left her. She couldn't just let herself blindly believe in a man again. No matter how cute he was.

"Yeah, I'm okay." She leaned her head back against the seat and closed her eyes. "I just wish I knew what was really going on."

"Me, too." Jeremy started the car and pulled out of the parking lot. "By the way, you look seriously sexy as Lara Croft. Could you keep that outfit and wear it for me again when all this is straightened out and you aren't looking at me as if I strangle kittens in my spare time?"

Maggie laughed. "Sorry. I just hate this. I want to believe you, Jeremy. I really do. But I'm a lawyer. I hear guilty people say they're innocent all the time."

Jeremy took her hand and squeezed it. "I know. I get it. And you can quote work stuff all day, but I know where this is really coming from and I'm not him, Maggie. I'm not your ex, and I'm not lying to you. I'm just as confused as you are about what's going on."

Maggie held his hand as if it were a lifeline, and she was afraid she might drown. She didn't want to lose this connection with him. She heard the sincerity in his voice, and she wanted to believe. She wanted to drink his Kool-Aid. Fill up her cup and ask for seconds. But she couldn't make that leap. She just wasn't ready to take a sip. "I'm trying, Jeremy."

"I know. That's all I ask." He switched lanes and set the cruise control. "Now that I have time to concentrate, tell me again what this Officer McCarthy told you. Start from the beginning and don't leave anything out. And since when does the Pleasant Valley Police Department make house calls?"

Maggie relayed their entire conversation to Jeremy. Well, she left out the part about him asking her to go for a ride on his motorcycle and fantasizing about him in leather chaps.

Jeremy tapped the steering wheel and moved his mouth from side to side, as if the combination of motions would help him to think. "She said we were at the Travel Inn? The one on the highway?"

"Yeah. Why?"

"I don't think I've been there in years. Why would she pick that spot instead of one where I might actually have been seen?"

Maggie had an idea. It was risky, but she wanted to know the truth, even if it hurt. "We drive right by it on our way back into town. Why don't we stop in and see if we can talk to the desk guy? See if he remembers seeing you?"

"He won't remember seeing me. I just told you, I wasn't there. But, that's a good idea. I'd like to talk to the guy who *claims* he saw me. Maybe he can help us get to the bottom of this."

Thirty minutes later, they pulled into the Travel Inn. Only a handful of cars were in the parking lot and Jeremy held the door for Maggie to enter the lobby. The motel's registration area opened into the restaurant, and Maggie could see the bar area from the desk.

"You folks need a room?" The desk clerk didn't bat an eye at their costumes. He probably saw all kinds of interesting things working here. He looked to be in his early twenties. His dark hair was greasy and in need of some shampoo, and he smelled like a combination of marijuana smoke and Taco Bell burritos.

"Actually, we're looking to talk to the desk clerk that was working last Friday night, probably around nine." Maggie used her official lawyer voice. "Were you working that night?"

The desk guy shrugged. "Nah. That'd be Scooter. He works the night shifts on the weekend. Is he in some kind of trouble?"

"No, of course not," Jeremy assured him. "We just want to talk to him. Do you know when this Scooter will be in next?"

He looked at his arm, as if expecting to see a watch there. "Pretty soon. I get off in about twenty minutes and he should be here to cover the desk."

"Thanks. We'll just wait in the bar." He turned to Maggie. "Can I buy you a drink?"

"Does it come with a shot of hand sanitizer?"

They walked into the restaurant, and Maggie recognized the woman sitting at the end of the bar, a short glass of clear bubbly liquid in front of her. Maggie waved and pulled Jeremy across the bar. "Hi, Lori."

Lori Waddle looked up from her drink, and her face broke into a wide grin. She looked the couple walking toward her up and down. "Hey, Maggie and Hot Star Wars Guy. Isn't it a little early for Halloween?"

Maggie plopped into the seat next to her. "It's a long story. Can I buy you a drink?"

"Nah. I don't drink anymore." Lori hefted her glass. "It's just 7Up, but I like the way it fizzes and the feel of the glass in my hand. I should be buying you a drink, though. Thanks for helping me out of the slammer."

Jeremy looked at Maggie quizzically, as if he couldn't quite figure out the friendly connection between these two women.

"It's no big deal. I just made a few calls." Maggie gestured toward Lori. "Jeremy, this is Lori Waddle.

We met at the police station the night I was waiting for you."

Jeremy leaned forward to shake Lori's hand. "Nice meeting you. Do you come here often?"

Lori looked from Jeremy to Maggie. "Is he for real? Did your boyfriend just try to pick me up? Is that why you're dressed like that? You guys are into some weird, kinky role-play stuff?"

"No!" Maggie and Jeremy cried together.

Maggie thought it was kind of cute how Jeremy's face was turning bright red from the blush that started at his neck and burned up to his ears. "No. We're dressed like this because we were up in Denver at a comic book convention. And Jeremy wasn't trying to pick you up. He was really asking if you are here often, because we're wondering if you may have seen a friend of ours here last weekend."

"I wasn't judging or anything. What two consenting adults do in their own time is their business, not mine." Lori's easy smile was back, and she winked at Jeremy, obviously enjoying the way he so easily blushed. "So, tell me about this friend. I'm in this very spot most every Friday and Saturday night. There's not much I miss around here."

Maggie could see the hotel registration desk from where they sat at the bar. "Our friend is in her late twenties, big blond hair, kind of curvy, dresses slutty."

Jeremy pulled out his phone and thumbed through his camera roll. "Here, I've got a picture of her in here somewhere."

Maggie gave him a look. "You have a picture of her? In your phone?"

Jeremy shrugged innocently. "What? It's from the Christmas party. Here it is." He turned the phone to Lori, and she squinted at the small screen.

A look of recognition crossed her face. "Oh yeah, I totally recognize this chick. She was here last weekend. I remember because she was laughing really loudly, and she was wearing this awful purple dress, and her girls looked like they were ready to pop out of the top of it."

Maggie nodded. "That's her all right. Was she with anyone?" *With a guy? One that looked like the guy standing next to me, but without the Jedi cape on?* She knew she couldn't ask. Leading the witness and all that, but she held her breath as she waited to hear Lori's answer. Her heart sank as Lori nodded her head.

"Yeah. She was with a guy. Blond hair, not real tall, kinda cute. But, he had that cocky thing about him, where he acted like he owned the joint. And kind of looked down his nose at this place, like he was better than it."

Jeremy's eyes widened. "Skyler? Was here with Charlotte? I can't believe it."

"I can." Maggie held out her hand. "Let me see your phone." She took Jeremy's phone and Googled "SkyVision CEO", looking for an image of Skyler. Finding one, she enlarged the photo and held it up to Lori. "Does this look like the guy?"

"Winner, winner, chicken dinner! That's him all right." Lori reached for her bag. "If you all keep showing me these pictures, I'm gonna have to get my reading glasses out."

"Don't bother. That's all we have." Maggie smiled at her unlikely friend. "You have helped us immensely."

"You're the one that's helped me." Lori leaned closer to Maggie. "I've got a job interview with your friend on Tuesday. Thanks for setting that up. I'm kind of nervous."

Maggie gave her an assuring smile. "Don't worry. It's just clerical stuff. Filing and answering phones. I'm sure you'll do great."

Jeremy tapped Maggie on the shoulder. "I think our friend just arrived for his shift."

Maggie turned to see another young, greasy-haired kid in baggy jeans and Converse tennis shoes replace the first guy at the hotel registration desk. "We gotta go, Lori. Let me know how the interview goes. And thanks for your help."

"Anytime."

Maggie and Jeremy approached the new desk clerk. His eyes were glazed over, and he welcomed them with the goofy smile of a true stoner. "Hey, dudes. What's up? Need a room?"

What was up with this place? Was a daily supply of happy grass part of their benefit package?

"Are you Scooter?" Jeremy asked.

"Yeah, who wants to know?"

"I'm just wondering if you recognize me?"

Maggie's heart sank as the clerk's face broke into a grin.

"Yeah, totally, dude. I just saw you last week."

Maggie gulped, afraid to ask the question, but knowing she had to hear the answer. "You saw him last week?"

Scooter nodded. "Yeah, they ran a whole *Star Wars* marathon on TV last week. I spent the whole day watching them."

Are you kidding? Maggie rolled her eyes and pointed at Jeremy. "No, I mean this guy in particular. Do you know who he actually is?"

Scooter looked at her as if she were the confused one. "Yeah, totally. I'm not an idiot."

Maggie waited. "Well, who is he?"

Scooter flashed a grin at Jeremy. "Only the best Jedi Knight in history, Obi Wan-Kenobi."

Maggie buried her head in her hands. Jeremy put a hand on her shoulder. "Let me try."

He took his Jedi cape off and draped it over his arm. "Okay, now I am just a guy. Can you tell us if you have ever seen me in person, here at the motel?"

Scooter squinted at Jeremy. "Nope. Sorry dude. Am I supposed to know you? Were you, like, one of my teachers in high school? 'Cause I smoked a lot of weed back then, and some of high school is a little blurry."

Back then? Like last week? Maggie took a deep breath, reigning in her patience. She was a lawyer and a mother of two teenage boys; she knew how to gain information. "Scooter, do you remember the police coming in and questioning you about some people you might have seen at the motel?"

He nodded. "Oh ya, totally. Big bald guy, serious cop. He was asking about some chick and her boyfriend that had checked in last week."

Jeremy held out his phone with the picture of Charlotte on it. "Do you recognize this woman? Is this the 'chick' he was asking about?"

Again, Scooter squinted at the small picture. Maybe he needed glasses. She could ask Lori if he could borrow hers. "Yeah, that's her. I remember her." He wiggled his eyebrows at Jeremy. "She was wearing this tight dress. I think it was like purplish, and it was totally low cut. She had this big blond hair and big…" He emphasized the last "big" and held his hands out as if he were juggling melons.

"We get the picture," Maggie snapped. "Was she alone or with someone else?"

"She was with a dude and he kept looking at her big…" More melon-juggling motions.

"All right, forget about her big…melons." *Geez, is this all men think about?* Maggie sighed and tried again. "What can you tell us about the guy?"

Scooter laughed. "Hey dudette, settle down. Don't be jealous." He eyed Maggie's snug black tank top. "Yours are nice too. I like the whole Lara Croft thing doing it with a Jedi idea."

Jeremy put a hand on Maggie's arm, holding her back from pulling one of her Lara Croft guns from their holster and using it on this guy. The guns didn't really shoot ammunition, but she could whap him upside the head with them. And she might have to whack Jeremy too, since he was grinning like a fool, as if he were enjoying this whole discussion.

And he should. Actually, she should be quite happy too. She should probably lean over and give old Scooter a hug. He had just cleared Jeremy's name. He had admitted that he hadn't seen him before and that Charlotte was lying when she said she spent the night here at the motel with him.

Jeremy was looking at her as if he were waiting for her to catch up. She nodded, and he turned back to Scooter. "So, this dude she was with. Did he look like me? Like regular me, not *Star Wars* me."

"Nah, dude. He was shorter and had blond hair. He was like a little squirly guy who acted like he was a big shot. I remember thinking I couldn't be too down on him, though, 'cause he gave me a big tip."

Jeremy flipped back to the picture of Skyler on his phone and held it out to Scooter. "Was this the guy?"

Scooter laughed. "Yeah, that's the little dude, all right."

Maggie was not sure what was so funny that this clerk kept laughing about. She guessed the laughter had more to do with the substance he smoked before showing up to work than the substance in the photograph. "Why did you tell the police that the guy she was with had dark hair?"

Scooter thought for a minute. "Did I? I don't remember. I guess 'cause I've seen her here before and that dude had dark hair."

Maggie's eyes widened. "You've seen her before? Checking into the motel, with a different man?"

"Yeah, she's been here a few times. I always remember a good set of..." He cupped his hands again.

Oh dear Lord, let's not start with the melons again. Maggie pointed at Jeremy. "Has she ever been in here with this guy?"

Scooter looked up at Jeremy. "Nope. I've never seen you before. You're pretty tall, dude. I would remember you."

"Thank you. I guess." Jeremy turned to Maggie. "What now?"

Maggie tapped her fingers on the registration counter, then held out her hand to Jeremy. "Do you have other pictures of that Christmas party? Let's show them to Scooter and see if he recognizes anyone else from the pictures."

"Good idea." Jeremy scrolled through the dozen or so pictures he had taken at the office party, showing them to Scooter, and scanning his face for a look of recognition.

Scooter pointed to one of the frames. "There. That's the dude. I've seen her with him a couple of times over the last several months."

Jeremy held the phone up to Maggie and showed her a picture of Charlotte, her arms draped over a dark-haired man. Maggie was expecting to see Jim Edwards, the man she had been dating the last six months. She drew in a quick breath, not prepared for the dark-haired man wearing a goofy grin to be Leonard Finch.

Half an hour later, Maggie and Jeremy pulled into her driveway. She reached for her purse, then remembered that she had given it to Cassie to take back to her car. They had left the motel, and Jeremy had insisted they stop at a cell phone store to replace her iPhone.

As tired as she was, she was glad they had made the stop. She hated being without her phone today. It had taken a few extra minutes for the sales-girl to get it all set up and explain how to load all of her previous info onto the new phone. Then the girl had insisted on taking their pictures, raving about how adorable they looked in their costumes.

Maggie felt anything but adorable right now. She felt hot and tired and wiped out from the crazy activity of the day. She looked up at Jeremy, who had come around the car and stood holding the car door open for her. He wore the same drained expression that she felt. "Thanks for bringing me home."

He pulled her from the car and into his arms. He held her against him in a tight embrace. As tired as she was, the pressure of his body and his voice at her ear sent goosebumps racing down her arms. "Thanks for not giving up on me. I don't know what's going on around here, but I know that I don't want to lose you."

Jeremy drew back and tipped her chin up to look at him. "As much as I want to find out what happened to Jim and what kind of crazy scheme is going on, the most important thing to me right now is you."

He couldn't possibly know how much those words meant to her. She had never felt like the most important thing to Chad. He had always been concerned about the house and the cars and the boys. She believed that he loved her, at one time. And he was a good dad to their boys. But she couldn't remember him ever looking her in the eye and telling her she was the most important thing to him.

She reached up and touched Jeremy's cheek. A light stubble had formed after the long day, and she brushed her fingers along the fine whiskers. She liked the way his face looked. His jaw was strong. His nose was narrow and just a little too long. His dark eyebrows framed his brown eyes, and as she looked into his eyes now, all she saw was affection reflected there.

Could she really take a chance on this man? Return that affection and risk being hurt again? She felt so good being in his arms. So right.

Especially when he ran his hands down her back like that. And dipped his head to lightly kiss her neck. And…oh forget it. She wrapped her arms around his neck and kissed him. Pressing her body against his and indulging in the pleasure of this moment. Of his mouth. His lips, his tongue. Of his hands pulling her closer to him. Of his hips against hers, the evidence of his want pressing against her.

Slamming the door behind her, he pushed them against the car, her back against the frame. He buried his face in her neck, his breath ragged. "You are so sexy. I love your hair and the way you smell. And this outfit on you is making me crazy. You are like a video game fantasy come to life."

She kissed his neck and nibbled his earlobe, loving the effect she was having on him. "I like being one of your fantasies." She wrapped her leg around his and teased him playfully. "Do you have any places you want me to explore? Any precious artifacts you want me to check out?"

Jeremy groaned. "You are killing me. It's bad enough you look just like Lara Croft, now you sound like her too." He laughed and pulled his hands back in an "I surrender" gesture. "I think we better stop. Or I'm gonna have to throw you down on the lawn and take serious advantage of you."

Maggie smiled. He was probably right. For a second, she entertained the thought of him laying down his Jedi cape on her lawn and showing her his light saber. But her neighbors probably wouldn't be as excited. Well, that one guy, in the brown house down the street, he would probably love it. He'd come out and take pictures.

She pulled away, missing the warmth of him, the feel of him already. "You're right. I should go in."

He drew her back once more, kissing her fully on the mouth, one hand tight against her back and the other cradling her head. He completed the kiss and leaned his forehead against hers. "Maggie, you mean everything to me. You fill up my thoughts and my dreams. You are always in my head. I think about you all day. I wake up in the morning and can't wait to call you. And I know as soon as I drive away tonight, I'll already be missing you. You make me crazy."

Maggie closed her eyes. "You make me pretty crazy too." She pulled back and headed across her lawn. She opened the front door and waved at Jeremy, who was still standing by the car, watching her walk away.

She sighed as she pushed the door closed behind her.

"It's about time you got home."

Maggie jumped and let out a little shriek, turning to see Chad sitting on the sofa in the living room, a book in his hand. "Holy crap, you scared me."

She put her hand to her rapidly beating heart. "And it doesn't matter when I get home. You're not my dad." *Or my husband. Anymore.*

She sank into the armchair across from him and waited as she heard Barney running from his bed in the kitchen to welcome her home. She held open her arms, and the dog jumped into her lap, licking her neck and face.

She greeted the dog with kisses and coos, then looked up at Chad. "What are you doing up, anyway?" She motioned to the book in his hands. "And since when do you like to read?"

Chad gestured to her outfit. "Since when do you like to role-play?"

"Since none of your business." She laughed inwardly at the shocked look that crossed her ex-husband's face and took a little satisfaction in surprising him. "But as far as this costume is concerned, it was purely for investigative purposes. We followed Jeremy up to this comic book convention thing in Denver, and we needed costumes as disguises."

"I know." Chad pointed to the loveseat, where her purse sat on top of the clothes she had on earlier that day. "Cassie and Piper dropped by earlier and told us about it. They wanted to drop off your purse, and I think Piper wanted Drew to see her costume."

"That was nice of them. Cassie is always thinking of us."

"She looked pretty hot in that Wonder Woman outfit. It was a new look for her. I think Matt's gonna be a happy man tonight."

Maggie laughed. He was probably right. Cassie did look pretty great in that outfit.

Chad wiggled his eyebrows at her. "And that's a pretty sexy look on you, too. You make a good Lara. Wanna raid my tomb?"

Oh, brother. This outfit consisted of a tank top and a pair of shorts. But throw on a pair of guns with thigh holsters and men couldn't think straight. She shook her head. "Uh, no."

He gave her a lecherous grin. "I'm around if you change your mind."

Time to change the subject. "So, what are you reading?" She ducked her head to see the cover. "Is that our book club book?"

He shrugged. "It's no big deal. I heard you guys talking about it and thought I would check it out. I kinda like it."

Before she could formulate a response, her new cell phone buzzed in her pocket. She pulled it out and grinned as she read the text from Jeremy: *Just made it home. Still thinking about you. Goodnight, Beautiful.*

Chad's light tone was replaced by one of annoyance. "Get a text from Loverboy?"

Maggie ignored Chad as her phone buzzed again. Expecting another text from Jeremy, she was surprised when the caller ID read *Unknown*. A shiver of terror ran down her spine, and the color drained from her face as she read the new message: *Keep your nose out of where it doesn't belong, or you could end up like Jim.*

"It was probably just a prank." Maggie took her new phone back from Cassie after showing her and Piper the threatening message. It was Sunday morning, and the wagons were circling around Maggie. She had called Sunny the night before to tell her about the message and Sunny had spurred the Page Turners into action.

The front door opened, and Sunny marched in. Edna was right behind her, a huge pink handbag slung over one arm and a pan of her famous cinnamon rolls in her hands. As the heady scent of freshly baked bread and cinnamon filled the room, Maggie's mouth watered in anticipation of the rolls.

As one unit, the group filed into the kitchen. Amidst excited chatter, plates and forks were dispensed and cups were filled with coffee. Drew had wandered into the kitchen and was met with a hug from Piper and a plate of cinnamon heaven, a yellow pat of butter melting in the middle of the roll.

They passed Maggie's phone around, and each read the message.

Sunny looked at the display then handed the phone to Edna. "And you called the police, right?"

"Only after I told her that if she didn't, I would," Chad said as he ambled into the kitchen and made his way to the coffeepot. "You guys want me to make waffles again?"

"No, thanks. Edna brought cinnamon rolls." Cassie scooped a gooey roll onto a plate and passed it to Chad, who took a seat in one of the bar stools at the counter.

Both Maggie and her friends were getting used to having Chad around again, and she wasn't exactly sure how she felt about that. But that was a question she would have to ponder later. Right now, they had bigger fish to fry. "Yes. I called Mac and told him about the message. But I got to thinking that maybe we could do some investigating on our own."

Edna pushed her empty plate back and rubbed her hands together. "Now you're talking. Tell me where to start. You want me to dust your phone for fingerprints?"

Maggie shook her head. *Was she kidding?* With Edna, it was hard to tell. "Of course not. The person sent me the message electronically. The only fingerprints that will be on it would be mine and Jeremy's. And every person in this room who's touched the phone."

"Good thinking," Edna said, not to be deterred by Maggie's comments. "How about I do some interrogating? Got anyone I can question?"

"Actually, that's not the worst idea. The police can try to track down who the call came from, but I can't imagine it's going to be that simple. No one would be dumb enough to send a message like that from their own phone." Maggie licked a dollop of white frosting from her thumb. "But I was thinking we could start digging into all the players. We can Google Jim and Charlotte and Skyler. And that nerdy Leonard guy. Even Jeremy. We can look up their past jobs, where they went to school, check out their Facebooks, see what they're tweeting. We need to see if we can find any kind of connection between them that might help us figure out who had the most to gain by Jim's death."

"Good idea, Mom. We can all help." Drew reached across Maggie and pulled another roll from the pan. "I'll bring my laptop and iPad out here for you guys while Piper and I look stuff up on our phones."

"I'll clean up in here and then use your PC in the office to search," Chad offered.

Did Chad just offer to clean up the kitchen? Who was this guy and what had he done with her ex-husband? The one who thought the dishwasher was run by estrogen.

They made quick work of setting up a command central in the kitchen. After Drew found a power-bar extension cord, they plugged in laptops, iPads, and Cassie's Kindle Fire. Cassie made a list of things to check out and assigned each person a specific area to check into.

Maggie unearthed a big poster board with one of the boy's old school projects on the back and taped it onto the wall of the dining area. She listed each of the names across the top: Jim, Charlotte, Leonard, Skyler, and Jeremy. Then she instructed the group to fill in information they found under each name.

By this time, Dylan had woken up, eaten a roll, and brought down a packet of multi-colored markers to use on the poster board. He and Chad retreated to Maggie's office to use her home computer.

The noise of the kitchen settled into a quiet hum as each person clicked and tapped, tracking down electronic rabbit holes as they dug for information. Motion stopped each time someone got up to fill in information on the poster board, each using that piece to either delete their path or to continue to search for another related thread of information.

Maggie saw that Sunny had listed Charlotte's graduation date from Coronado High School in Colorado Springs. She Googled their online yearbook for that year and began to search the classmates and class pictures.

Bingo! She couldn't believe it. Maggie waved the group over and pointed to a picture of a blond-haired boy with braces and a bad haircut. "Look at this. In the senior pictures of Charlotte's graduating class is a picture of Skyler Humphries. They went to high school together."

"Nice work, Mags," Sunny said. "But there were hundreds of kids in that school. Just because they were in the same class doesn't prove they knew each other."

"No, but this does." Piper turned her iPad to show the group the grainy black-and-white photograph of Charlotte and Skyler standing next to each other, each with a hand on a beaker of white liquid in front of them. The caption below the picture read: "Chemistry Club takes award in State Finals."

The doorbell rang, and Maggie heard Dylan yell he would get it. "So, now we know for sure that Charlotte and Skyler knew each other from high school. But, if they were so close, why didn't she go to work for SkyVision? Why work for Jeremy?"

"Unless," Sunny answered, "she was a plant all along, and she's only been working there to spy on the competition and feed SkyVision their new technology. But how can we prove if she's being loyal to Jeremy or still connected to Skyler?"

"That's a great question. We've been working on that ourselves." Officer McCarthy stood in the doorway of the kitchen, surveying the command post and the poster full of colored notes. "But if I had known you all were going to do our work for us, we could have all gone out for coffee."

"And donuts." Edna had been in the living room on the phone, so she squeezed past Mac and stepped into the kitchen. "I know cops really like donuts."

Mac sighed. "I think a lot of people really like donuts, Miss Allen. As far as I know, cops do not have the market cornered on donut eating."

Maggie pointed to the pan of rolls on the counter. "We don't have donuts, but Edna makes an amazing cinnamon roll. Have a seat, and I'll bring you one. How do you like your coffee?"

"Black. And I don't want to perpetuate the cliché of cops and donuts, but a cinnamon roll sounds great." Mac winked at Maggie, then crossed the room and scanned the notes they had printed on the board. "You guys do pretty good work. You dug up some things even my guys didn't find. I can see why you're looking into Jeremy's alibi and his competition, but why are you digging up info on this Leonard guy? What does he have to do with anything?"

Maggie handed Mac a cup of coffee and a cinnamon roll. He took an empty seat at the kitchen table and listened intently as the Page Turners filled him in on their adventures at Comic Con and Maggie and Jeremy's visit to the Travel Inn.

"Thank you for the roll. It lived up to its claim of amazing." Mac smiled at Edna, then scraped the last bite of roll onto his fork and scooped it into his mouth. "It sounds like you all have been pretty busy. I have to admit, I'm impressed with your work here. And I would have paid money to see you in those costumes."

"I've got pictures," Piper said.

"You do?" Maggie turned to the younger girl. "When did you take pictures?"

Piper shrugged. "All afternoon. I had my phone and there were so many crazy things at the conference, I took a bunch of pictures. I took this great one of you and Aunt Cassie at lunch."

Mac dug a business card out of his front pocket and passed it to Piper. "Can you email me all the photos?" He smiled up at Maggie. "I would like to see a picture of you in this Lara Croft outfit. But on a more professional note, I can have my guys look the pictures over and see if they can find anything in the background or pick up anything suspicious from the photos."

"Like a picture of Leonard," Maggie said. "I don't know how long he was up there, but Jeremy and I saw him right after we ate lunch. He was wearing a Superman costume."

Mac scribbled some notes on a small notebook he pulled from his pocket. "You never know what you might have got a shot of by accident." He motioned to the poster board. "Mind if I copy down some of this stuff you found?"

"Knock yourself out." Maggie took a marker from the table and added the Chemistry Club connection to the list under Charlotte and Skyler's names.

Mac wrote the last piece down. "That's actually a really interesting bit of information. We're waiting for the tox screen on the poison that killed our victim, but with a bit of a chemistry background, it's pretty easy to create an array of poisons that could be used to kill someone."

"Oh, poo." Edna poured herself another cup of coffee. "I don't know chemistry from biology, but I could make a poison to kill someone. Take a cup of bleach, pour in some rat poison and a little 409 and voila, you're dead."

Mac nodded. "Well, sure, anyone *could* make a cup of poison. But no one would drink it. To make something to put into someone's drink that is odorless and tasteless, that takes some skill. And remind me never to have coffee at your house." He shook his head and muttered, "And a little 409."

"I'll have you know that I make excellent coffee. You're welcome to stop by anytime and have a cup whenever you need help discussing a case," said Edna. "And I have another piece of information to add to the board."

"What information?" Maggie asked. "You weren't even online. I heard you in the living room talking on the phone."

"You have your ways of finding stuff and I have mine." Edna tapped Mac on the shoulder and pointed to his notebook. "You might want to write this down, Mac. I saw Piper post that Leonard listed his hometown as Greeley, Colorado, on his Facebook page. That's a pretty small town and just a few hours from here. I remembered that I took a water aerobics class with a gal from there, which by the way, water aerobics is really good for your joints if you're interested. Anyway, I called her and asked her if she knew the family. Well, she didn't know them personally, but she knew where the family lived, and she used to play bridge with a gal named Agnes who lived on the same street. I used to play bridge fairly often, but one of the gals in our foursome kicked the bucket and we just couldn't find anyone to replace her. So I called Agnes, and wouldn't you know, she'd lived on that street for years and used to babysit Leonard and his sister."

Maggie smacked her forehead with her hand. "Do you have a cup of that bleach poison lying around? I might need a sip. For the love of all that is holy, could you please get to the point?"

Edna huffed. "Just hold your cotton-pickin' horses. I'm getting to it. So Agnes, who seems like just a delightful woman, by the way." She raised her eyebrows at Maggie, daring her to say something. Maggie dropped her head to the table in an exaggerated smack.

Edna continued, ignoring her friend's theatrics. "So, Agnes said that earlier this winter, around the holidays, Leonard was home and talking about a woman that he was seeing. He told his mother, who then told Agnes, how much he liked this woman and thought they had a real future. He seemed quite enamored with her." Edna paused for effect. "She said that he brought her home one weekend, and Agnes described her as a blonde who showed off way too many of her curvy assets and looked a bit like a hussy to her."

Well, that described Charlotte all right. Maggie picked up a red marker and added "Dated the hussy, Charlotte" to their information board under Leonard's name. "So, she must have dated Leonard before she started seeing Jim."

"It sounds to me like this woman gets around," Mac said.

Edna tapped his notebook. "It sounds to me like you need to talk to her again and see just how many of these men she has had relations with. And you know what I mean by *relations*."

Mac rolled his eyes. "Yes, I know what you mean. And you might be right. Not about the relations business, but I think I will talk to her again. It sounds like she might know a little more than she's been letting on." He looked at Maggie. "But if she's dated half the single guys at Jeremy's company, what makes you so sure she hasn't had *relations* with the boss himself?"

Great question. Maggie gulped. "Because he told me he didn't."

Mac's gaze was unrelenting, and Maggie felt sorry for those he had in the interrogating room. "And you trust him?" he asked.

Trust him? Why did he have to use *that* word? Did she *trust* him? Depended on which day you asked her.

Or which hour. Or minute. She returned Mac's stare. "I believe him. And besides, we already know that Charlotte is a liar. She lied about the alibi and being with Jeremy in the motel."

Mac tapped his fingers on the table. "That one has me stumped. I was going to send a guy out to verify that story, but I think I'll go out to the Travel Inn myself and speak to this Scooter fellow."

Maggie tapped the poster board. "And now we know she also has another strong connection with Jeremy's competition. It wouldn't surprise me if *she* was the one who sent me that text."

"Have you run a trace on that text yet? Do we know who sent it?" Edna asked.

Mac shook his head at her. "I don't know who this 'we' is. But my guy ran it down and we don't know who it's from. It was sent from a burner phone."

"What's a burner phone?" Sunny asked.

"It's like a pay-as-you-go phone," Edna answered. "Anyone can buy one and pay to put minutes on it but there's no contract, so they stay anonymous."

Sunny raised her eyebrows at Edna. "How do *you* know what a burner phone is?"

Edna shrugged. "What? I watch *Castle*. Someone's always using a burner phone on that show."

"She's actually right." Mac stood, shoving his notebook back into his pocket. "Now, if you ladies will excuse me, I need to get back to work. Thanks for the cinnamon roll and the coffee. They were delicious." He looked directly at Maggie. "You have my number. Let me know if you get another text or if you feel threatened in any way. I don't want anything to happen to you."

Maggie swallowed and nodded her head, the heat level in his gaze causing her mouth to go dry and her palms to sweat.

He held her with his look for a moment longer. "I'll show myself out. You ladies stay out of trouble." He pointed at Edna. "Especially you." Then he was gone.

The book club stared at each other for a moment, speechless in his absence. Then Cassie picked up a napkin and fanned herself. "Is it warm in here?"

"Holy testosterone," Sunny said, turning to Maggie. "That man is hot with a capital H! And he is totally into you."

Maggie waved her away and turned back to the poster board. "I don't need him to be into me. I need him to figure out who killed Jim Edwards. And I need it not to have been Jeremy." She picked up a marker and snapped the cap off. "There was one more piece of information that I discovered in my internet search."

"Why didn't you tell Mac?" Sunny asked.

"Because it wouldn't have helped Jeremy." Still holding the marker, Maggie placed it under Jeremy's column and wrote, "Graduated college with a degree in Computer Engineering and a minor in *Chemistry*."

The doorbell rang, and Maggie checked her image in the mirror hanging from her bedroom closet door. She had picked a long blue dress to wear on her date with Jeremy tonight. The dress was strapless and showed off her tanned shoulders. The flowing fabric hugged her slim figure, and the V-necked bodice draped low across her chest and clung seductively to her breasts.

She had picked a simple pair of silver sandals that accented her denim-colored toenail polish. A blue amethyst pendant on a silver chain hung around her neck and dipped into her cleavage. Thanks to good genes and a great push-up bra, Charlotte was not the only one who had a great pair of assets.

Maggie loved the excited feeling of butterflies in her stomach she still got when she knew she was going to see Jeremy. She adored the smile that crossed his face when he saw her, and thrilled that his smile was just for her. She loved the way he seemed to drink her in with his eyes. He made her feel beautiful and special.

Now, if only she could get the idea of him in a white lab coat mixing up a beaker of deadly poison for his employee out of her mind, she would feel so much better about this date.

She stepped into the hall and ran into Chad coming out of Dylan's bedroom.

Chad looked her up and down, making no disguise of his approval of her outfit. "Wow! You look good enough to eat. Hot date with Nerdville tonight?"

Maggie sighed. "Yes, I have a date with Jeremy tonight. I heard the doorbell, so I assume he's downstairs waiting."

Chad stepped back. "Don't let me hold you back." He didn't step completely out of the way, standing just close enough that Maggie had to brush past him on her way downstairs. He ran his hand down her back as she passed him. "Have a fun time."

A shiver ran down Maggie's spine as she walked down the stairs. What kind of game was Chad playing? Why was he giving her compliments and touching her back? She now knew not to trust him. That guy always had an angle.

All thoughts of Chad left her mind as she saw Jeremy standing in her living room.

He wore expensive jeans, black dress shoes, and a slim black button-up shirt. He held a bouquet of three purple long-stemmed calla lilies tied in a white satiny ribbon. The smile she had been hoping for was absent from his face, replaced with a look of wonder instead.

Jeremy shook his head as she approached him. He picked up her hand and laid a kiss on the inside of her palm, then looked deeply into her eyes. "Maggie, you take my breath away. You look stunning."

Oh. My.

Maggie swallowed at the emotion threatening to spill from her. Tears filled her eyes and those butterflies were doing insane loop-de-loops in her stomach. A tiny finger of fear crept in as she realized how much she was falling for this man.

This man who brought her purple calla lilies instead of roses. She had told him once that calla lilies were her favorite flowers. That she loved the elegance of them. And he had listened and remembered.

His words made her feel like a treasure. Like she was adored. She thought of Chad's comment on her looking good enough to eat. Being described as "stunning" beat a comparison to an entrée any day.

She reached up to hug him, breathing in the intoxicating scent of his aftershave.

A wave of desire ran down her spine as he whispered in her ear. "I missed you."

"I missed you too." Maggie looked into his eyes and saw her own feelings reflected there. "It's been a long week."

Maggie took the flowers into the kitchen in search of a vase. This week had seemed long. She hadn't seen Jeremy since he dropped her off after Comic Con. They had spoken on the phone, but her days had been filled with work and Dylan's two soccer games. Jeremy was caught up in his own busy schedule and hadn't been able to get away to attend either of the games.

Chad had gone with her, and though she was glad for Dylan that his dad was at his games, she was still uneasy about the kids depending too much on their dad's presence. She didn't want to see her sons get hurt again.

She had to give Chad credit for attending the games and spending more time with the boys since he'd been back. He did seem different. Could a midlife affair with a Hooters waitress who took all his money and then ditched him have taught him to appreciate the life he had before? The one he had so carelessly thrown away?

Maggie hoped so. It would serve him right. She hated the bitter feeling that burned like acid in her stomach whenever she thought of Chad deserting her and their marriage for a younger woman. She hated the way that acid charred any attempt she made at finding love again. Searing the edges of her heart, destroying any hope of letting new love in.

She placed the flowers in a vase and put Chad out of her mind, determined to focus on Jeremy and their date tonight. Pushing back the resentment and bitterness, she set the vase on the table, grabbed her purse, and stepped back into the living room. Taking Jeremy by the arm, she smiled up at him. "Let's go have some fun."

Maggie pushed her plate back, amazed that she had eaten the whole hunk of lasagna. The clingy dress didn't seem like such a great idea now. After a meal of lasagna and breadsticks, she could use a pair of stretchy-denim jeans, some Spanx, and a top she could untuck to hide her bloated belly.

"Feel like dessert?" Jeremy eyed her empty plate. "They have a pretty good cheesecake here."

She was already bloated and full, but that cheesecake did sound good. What could another twelve hundred calories hurt? "Sure. I'll split a piece with you."

They had kept their discussion light all evening, but now Maggie tried to think of an easy way to slip the topic of Jim's murder into the conversation. She wanted to know if Jeremy knew anything more or if he had heard from Charlotte. "Sooo, hear anything new on Jim's murder?"

That was about as subtle as a bull in a china shop.

"Not really. Everyone at work is in such a state of stress. We're still under deadline to get this new game out, and everyone is still grieving for Jim. I think the staff is divided between thinking his murderer was someone we work with or an outsider. And there are a few of my employees who are still looking at me kind of strangely, as if they suspect that I am the murderer and they could be the next victim."

"How about Charlotte? How is she treating you?" *Good job, Maggie. That bull is just dancing around doing a subtlety jig now, knocking down china left and right.*

"Charlotte hasn't shown up for work this week. She's still doing her work, but sending it in via email and by computer. She's worked from home before, but this is really strange. She's not answering any of my calls or texts, but she is keeping up on all of her work."

"Jeremy, I have to tell you something." Maggie wiped her sweaty palms on the cloth napkin in her lap. She knew she needed to admit to him the Page Turners were looking into the murder, but she was worried that Jeremy wouldn't appreciate what they had found. "The book club was over last weekend, and we got to digging around on the internet, and we found some strange connections."

"Strange how?"

"Strange, like did you know that Charlotte and Skyler went to high school together? They knew each other and were in Chemistry Club together. Charlotte could be the one that's leaking information to Skyler. And their knowledge of chemistry gives them the means to have created a poison."

"Just because they were in Chemistry together doesn't mean they created a murderous potion. I have a background in chemistry, too. In fact, I minored in it in college." He looked at Maggie and realization crossed his face. "But you already knew that, didn't you?"

He took Maggie's hands in his. "Listen Maggie, just because I am skilled in chemical equations doesn't mean I would have the means or knowledge to create a deadly poison. It basically means that I have the periodic table memorized and know the chemical name for salt is sodium chloride."

Maggie smiled. "I feel like the chemistry piece is just one more nail in the coffin for you. First, you gave Jim all that money, and then this chemistry thing and the fact that Charlotte has cast doubt on your alibi. It all adds up to not a very positive tally in your Innocent Scorecard."

Jeremy gave her a quizzical look. "How do you know that I gave Jim a bunch of money?"

"Mac told me on the same day that he informed me about your alibi. I guess the information about you in a motel room with another woman overshadowed the money thing, and we never really got around to talking about it."

"Well, that Mac is just a wealth of information, isn't he?" The muscle in Jeremy's cheek flinched as he clenched and unclenched his jaw. He took a deep breath. "Maggie, Jim was one of my best employees. He was instrumental in helping me create this new game. I treat my employees very well. I told him if he finished ahead of time, that I would reward him with a bonus. He worked his butt off, putting in long hours, working on the weekends. And he produced the code we needed a week earlier than expected. The ten-thousand-dollar bonus I gave him was a drop in the bucket to the hundreds of thousands he saved us by coming in ahead of schedule."

Maggie nodded. The cheesecake arrived but sat untouched in the center of the table between them. "I told Mac there had to be a reasonable explanation for why you gave Jim the money. But that doesn't explain why he deposited twenty-five thousand from SkyVision."

Jeremy's mouth dropped open. "What? Did Mac tell you that too? I haven't heard anything about this. There's no reason for him to be getting paid anything from SkyVision." He closed his eyes and sighed in defeat. "Unless Jim was taking a payoff to sell Skyler our code. Damn it! I trusted that guy."

Maggie's heart went out to Jeremy. She knew all about having her trust broken. "Could there be another explanation? And how does Charlotte fit into this? She's the one with the connection to Skyler, not Jim.

But she *was* dating Jim. Could she have been coercing him to take a bribe?"

"I don't see how she could *coerce* him to do anything? She's five foot six."

Maggie raised her eyebrows at Jeremy. "Really? She has a lot of other forms of coercion that don't involve physical force. They might involve another kind of physical, though."

"Hmm. I see your point." He ran his fingers through his hair. "I just hate this feeling of not knowing what's going on in my own company. I feel like there's this elaborate joke that's being played, and I'm the butt of it, but I don't know why. Jim was with me for ten years. Why would he turn on me?"

"Sex and money are both very powerful motivators." Maggie picked up a fork and sliced the rectangular tip off the end of the cheesecake. "And all we're doing is guessing. We don't know for sure that Jim betrayed you or that Charlotte is in bed, so to speak, with SkyVision. This is all just supposition."

"You're right. I'm just tired of guessing. I want to *know* what's going on." Jeremy picked up the other fork and took a bite of the cheesecake. "I did try to shake things up a little at the office today."

"What do you mean?"

"Look, I hate thinking that someone at my office is involved in this. But if they are, I want to flush them out. Make them think that we're on to them. So they make a mistake or do something to show their hand."

"So, what did you do?"

"During the staff meeting today, I let it 'accidentally' slip that the police were closing in on a suspect. That they had found evidence to implicate someone and were getting close to making an arrest. It was all a bunch of bull, but I saw them use the same idea on *Law & Order* once, and it worked for them."

Maggie laughed. "Now you sound like Edna. Did she put you up to this?"

"No, but it does sound like something she would try." Jeremy took the last bite of cheesecake and signaled for the waiter to bring them their check. "I'm just tired of sitting around and doing nothing, waiting for the other shoe to fall. If this helps to flush them out, then great. I just don't want someone else to get hurt while we're waiting for the police, or the Page Turners Book and Detective Club, to figure it out."

Twenty minutes later, they were driving down the highway on the way back to Jeremy's house. The night was still warm, and they had the air conditioner on and the radio tuned to an oldies station. Jeremy was singing and teasing Maggie, trying to get her to sing along.

They were on the stretch of road between town and Jeremy's subdivision where traffic was typically light. In fact, they were the only car on the road. The moon was bright, and Maggie noticed how it reflected off the water as they approached the bridge that crossed the lake.

Jeremy playfully nudged her ribs as he sang an old Beatles tune. "Come on, Maggie. I know you know the words." He glanced in the rearview mirror. "What the heck? Check out this guy. He's in a heck of a hurry."

Maggie glanced behind them at the headlights that were approaching at breakneck speed. She turned back and automatically scanned the highway, checking to see if he had enough range to pass them. "This is a no passing zone, but I bet that jerk is going to try."

Jeremy slowed down. "Let him. I'm in no hurry. I'd rather have him pass me. Going that fast, he's going to kill somebody."

Jeremy couldn't have known how accurate his statement was.

Maggie's head jerked back to gauge the speed of the oncoming car. It flew up on them, not slowing or pulling into the left lane to pass. "Something's not right, Jeremy."

No sooner had she said the words than the car rammed into the back of Jeremy's 4Runner. Maggie and Jeremy were thrown forward, the seatbelt cutting into Maggie's bare shoulder with the force of the impact.

Maggie screamed as the car rammed them again. She looked to Jeremy.

His concentration was divided between holding the wheel steady and darting glances at the rearview mirror. "What the hell is wrong with this guy?"

The car moved into the left lane, speeding up to come even with them. Maggie caught a brief glimpse of the dark-colored sedan. She registered that the car was big and sturdy and thought with relief that he was finally going to pass them. She felt Jeremy ease up on the gas to let him get ahead of them before they hit the bridge.

Instead, the car jerked sideways, ramming Jeremy's truck and forcing them off the road. Jeremy yanked the wheel back, fighting for control of the car. The other car rammed them again, this time with more force. The 4Runner lost its traction and careened off the side of the road.

Unfortunately, they had just hit the edge of the bridge, and there was no pavement for them to land on. The car sailed off the edge of the road. Maggie screamed again as they held a moment in free fall before the car hit the water and plummeted into the lake.

Panic gripped her heart, like nothing Maggie had ever felt before. She could smell the algae as the murky green water rushed up the floor boards and submerged her feet. She gasped for breath as claustrophobia threatened to smother her. The water was coming in fast, and she fought against the dark borders that loomed on the edges of her vision, a clear indication that she was on the verge of blacking out.

A hand reached for hers, and she gripped it like a lifeline. Jeremy was there. She looked to him, already struggling for breath in the precious air left in the truck.

Jeremy squeezed her hand, his voice loud and strong. "Maggie. Focus on my voice. Take a deep breath. I've got you."

She nodded her head, quick bobs of understanding and tried to slow her breathing. Her thoughts went to Dylan and Drew. She could see them clearly as toddlers. A vision of the three of them cuddling on the sofa reading a book flashed across her mind. She could almost feel the soft cotton of their footy pajamas and smell the shampoo of their freshly washed hair.

She envisioned Drew in a tuxedo, a man on his wedding day. A day she might never see. Flashes of Dylan scoring a goal, a euphoric grin on his face. She had to see that face again. She prayed for strength and willed her breathing to slow.

"Good girl. That's it, Maggie. We've got to get your seatbelt off." He had already released his and was holding himself against the steering wheel so as not to fall into the windshield as the heavy engine dragged the hood of the car forward into the murky depths of the lake. He reached for her seatbelt and clicked the button. "Brace yourself, Maggie so you don't fall forward."

The belt released and she braced herself against the dashboard, her blue dress swirling in the water as it filled the car. The cold water was now up to her knees. "What do we do? Should I try to call 911?"

Jeremy shook his head. "There's no time. We have to roll the window down and swim out. The electric windows should still work." He reached across her and opened the glove box, pulling out a small yellow device that looked like a cross between a miniature hammer and a gun. "If they don't work, this will break the window. My mom saw this Oprah show about escaping a car filled with water and bought these for my brother and me."

Of course she did. Because that's what mothers do. They protect their kids. But how could Maggie protect hers if she wasn't around? She couldn't let that happen. She took a deep breath and steeled herself for their escape. "Okay. What do we do?"

"Can you crawl over the seat? We're going to try to get out the back window."

"Should we wait for the car to fill with water and try to get the door open?" The panic gripped her chest again as she imagined holding her breath as the water covered her and trying to maneuver the heavy door.

"There's no time. And I want us out of here before the car fills completely with water. Put your foot on the steering wheel and push yourself into the back seat." He grabbed her legs and guided her over the center console.

A pack of mints and one of her sandals floated in the water as it rose higher along the seat line. The car was nearly vertical in its descent and Jeremy pushed himself over the driver's seat.

Water poured into every crevice. It had been less than a minute since they hit the water, and it was already up to Maggie's waist. She could see the dim outline of the headlights as they shone through the greenish-blue layers of the lake.

Jeremy steadied himself against the window and took her face in his hand. His voice rang with a steely determination, and Maggie drew from his strength as he spoke. "Maggie, listen to me. We are going to get out of this car. I will not let anything happen to you. Are you listening?"

She nodded again, briskly shaking her head up and down, her teeth now chattering. She wasn't sure if it was from the cold lake water or the panic returning. "I'm listening."

Jeremy pushed against the back windshield of the 4Runner. "I'm gonna get this window open, one way or another. And when I do, the water is gonna come in fast. I want you to push off the back seat with your feet and push against the current. Swim up and out as hard as you can. Do you understand?"

"Y-y-yes." Her teeth were chattering harder. The murky green water entirely filled the bottom half of the car and she could no longer even see the front seats. "What about you?"

"Don't worry about me. You just swim with everything you have in you. I'll be right behind you. I just found you, and I refuse to let anything happen to you." He gripped her face and leaned in and gave her a hard kiss, filled with desperation and passion.

She felt his strength and determination come through that kiss. She filled herself up on it, kissing him back with a need so strong it almost overwhelmed her. A desperate plea to convey all of her feelings into that one moment, that one intimate crush of their lips.

The kiss lasted only a moment, but a lifetime of emotion was expressed in the delivery. Jeremy broke the connection and pressed his cheek to hers. "I love you, Maggie, and I'm gonna get you out of here."

Tears coursed down Maggie's face as she looked at Jeremy. This man whom she battled against her heart to trust and who was now fighting to save her life. "I believe you."

She did believe him. And she believed *in* him. The water was up to their chests, and she struggled to keep her breathing calm. But amidst the panic, despite the swirling water, Maggie had one perfect moment of clarity. Her brain shut down and her heart spoke the truth. In that moment, she knew. "I love you too."

Jeremy nodded. "You ready? It's gonna happen fast." He pushed the button to lower the back windshield. It whirred, but nothing happened. "Damn it!" He beat against the windshield. "I'm gonna have to break it." He looked at Maggie. "Hold your breath and swim as hard as you can."

She took a deep breath. "Do it!"

Jeremy pushed the tool against the window and pulled the trigger. With a pop, the glass shattered to pieces and all hell broke loose. The windshield broke inward with the force of the water and the lake came rushing forward in a current of green water filled with debris and chunks of the smashed windshield.

Maggie pushed off from the back seat, using all of her strength to push against the power of the rushing water. Her left arm and her bare leg scraped against the broken glass rimming the windshield frame as she swam through. She pushed her foot against the outer edge of the vehicle, gaining more momentum against the dominant strength of the water.

Her lungs felt at capacity, the crushing weight of water working against her as she flailed her arms and kicked with all of her might. She prayed she was swimming to the surface, the black night giving no aid in helping to determine the direction of the lake.

She knew she was at her limit, her lungs threatening to burst, her strength depleted. She had nothing left to give. An image of her sons flashed across her mind, the memory of their smiles spurring her on. She prayed and summoned every ounce of energy she had left. She kicked once more and broke free of the surface.

Gasping for breath, she splashed around in the water, calling Jeremy's name. From somewhere in the darkness, she heard a woman yelling, calling to her, but all she cared about was finding Jeremy. Why hadn't he surfaced? He was right behind her.

A new terror seized her. No longer afraid for her life, she was terrified that something had happened to his. Panic-filled images of what could have happened to him flooded her mind. She screamed his name, fear gripping her very soul.

What if he had hit his head on the car and been knocked unconscious? What if his clothes had snagged on the car and it was pulling him to his death, unwilling to release him as it sank to the lake floor? What if?

Relief flooded her as she heard a splash, and Jeremy's dark-haired head broke the surface of the water. He sputtered out lake water, choking as he called for her. "Maggie!"

She swam to him, tears of joy streaming down her cheeks, mixing with the water from the lake. "I'm here. Jeremy, I'm here."

Then he was there. Wrapping his arms around her, buoying her up, still thinking about her safety above his own. "Maggie. Thank God you're all right."

And she was all right. They both were. She kissed his face, awkwardly treading water and trying to hug him at the same time. "I'm so glad you're okay. You didn't come up, and I thought something…I thought you were…"

"It's okay. I'm okay." He gripped her shoulder, turning her toward the shore, where they could see someone waving their arms and calling to them. "Let's get out of this damn lake."

Pulling the scratchy wool blanket around her shoulders, Maggie stepped closer to Jeremy and tried not to shiver. The late-summer night air was still warm, but her clothes were soaking wet and clung to her goose-pimpled skin. The blanket had come from the car trunk of the woman who had been standing on the shore of the lake calling to them, and it smelled vaguely of horses.

Her name was Rita, and she claimed she had been a ways behind them on the highway when a dark-colored car sped past her and nearly ran her off the road. She saw it speed up on Jeremy's SUV and then ram it before running them off the road. It wasn't until she got closer that she saw they had plunged into the lake. She saw the back end of their car as it was sinking and had called 911.

She was standing on the side of the lake with a couple of blankets as Maggie and Jeremy swam to shore and waded out of the lake. Two police cars pulled up to the bridge, their lights flashing a red-and-blue strobe in the night sky.

Maggie was surprised to see Mac was one of the policemen. The look on his face as he rushed toward her told her that he was surprised to see her as well. "Maggie? What happened? Are you all right?"

"Some idiot ran them off the road," Rita answered, rubbing Maggie's shoulder. "I saw their car go into the lake, and I about had a heart attack. I couldn't believe it when I saw them both pop up out of that water. They're lucky to be alive."

Mac's eyes widened. "You were in the car while it was sinking?"

Maggie nodded. "We both were. Jeremy saved us. He broke the back window and got us out of the car." She pressed closer to the warmth of Jeremy's body as she looked up at him and smiled. "Thank goodness Jeremy's mom watches Oprah."

Mac looked at her questioningly.

"She saw an episode of Oprah that taught how to get out of a car submerged in water and bought Jeremy one of those tools that breaks out a window," Maggie explained. "That's how we got out."

The police officer shook his head. "Well, I'm glad you got out safely, but my main concern right now is how you got *in* there in the first place. Any idea who did this?"

Jeremy frowned at Officer McCarthy. "I was going to ask you the same thing."

"Did you get a good look at the vehicle? Could you see the driver? Was it someone you recognized?" Mac asked.

"No, it happened so fast. All I know is the car was a dark color. It was big and heavy enough to push us off the highway when it rammed into the side of us."

Jeremy shrugged. "That's about all I can tell you. It was dark, and the car just came out of nowhere. It flew up behind us and butted the back of my car a couple of times, then I thought it was going to pass us, but instead it ran us off the road and into the lake."

Mac turned to Maggie. "Did you see anything? Could you see the driver at all? Could you tell if it was a man or a woman?"

A woman? The thought hadn't crossed Maggie's mind that a woman could have done this. The only woman she could think of that might want to harm them hadn't shown up to work this week. Maggie had no idea what kind of car she drove. Though she pictured the blond bombshell in something small and sportier. And probably red.

Maggie shook her head. "I didn't see any more than Jeremy did. It happened like he said. One minute we were driving along, listening to the radio—the next, some asshole is crashing into us, and we were soaring into the lake." She shuddered at the memory of the car sinking into the water.

"All right. I'll call some divers and a wrecking crew in from Denver tomorrow. See if they can recover the car and tell us anything." Mac pointed at his squad car. "There's not much more we can do tonight. You can wait in my car. At least get the heat turned on."

Thirty minutes later, Mac pulled up in front of Maggie's house. Even though it was close to eleven, every light was blazing. The front door opened, and Chad and Maggie's sons came running out. She was surprised to see Sunny, Cassie, and Piper following close behind them.

Maggie pushed open the car door and ran for her boys, wrapping both of them in her arms and breaking into tears. Mac had found a gray hooded sweatshirt in his car and given it to Maggie to put on. The sleeves were too long but she didn't care. She was so glad to have her sons in her arms.

Dylan wouldn't let go of her, his arms clinging tightly to her middle, but Drew stepped back to look at her. "Mom, are you all right? We heard that your car crashed into the lake."

"It did. But we're okay. Jeremy saved us."

Jeremy stood next to the police car. His clothes were still damp, and he had lost both of his shoes in the lake. Drew took three steps and engulfed Jeremy in a huge bear hug, clapping him on the back. Maggie was surprised to see that her son was close to Jeremy's height. When had he grown into a man? If she hadn't already been crying, this emotional scene would have brought her to tears.

A moment later she was surrounded by her friends, each one hugging her and asking if she was okay. Chad waited behind her girlfriends, giving them each a chance to touch her and see that she was safe. Jeremy had stepped onto the lawn, and the women each took a turn hugging him too.

Maggie smiled as she saw Cassie move around the front of the police car to throw her arms around Mac, who was standing by the car.

"You scared me, Maggie-May." Maggie was surprised at the emotion she heard in Chad's voice as he pulled her into a tight hug. "You sure you're all right?"

She was touched by Chad's concern and nodded into his chest before letting him go. "I'll be better when I've washed the lake water out of my hair and put some dry clothes on. What is everyone doing here?"

Chad shrugged. "I got a call from the police that you had been in an accident. I was home playing video games with Dylan. We called Drew, who was with Piper at Cassie's house, and she must have called Sunny. I'm not really sure how it happened. All of a sudden, they were just all here."

Sounded about right. Maggie looked over his shoulder. "Where's Edna?"

"She's not here. I guess Sunny didn't want to wake her." Chad smiled. "You know there's gonna be hell to pay when she realizes she missed out on all this excitement."

Maggie laughed. Chad was right. "Well, all of this 'excitement' has about done me in. I just want a hot shower and my warm bed and about ten hours of sleep." She turned to find Jeremy behind her, and she wondered if his closeness had anything to do with Chad's embrace.

She wrapped her arms around Jeremy's waist, hugging him tightly. "Thanks for dinner. Oh, and for saving my life." She pushed up on her tip-toes to lay a light kiss on his lips. "I'll call you in the morning."

He squeezed her back. "Get some rest. We'll talk tomorrow. Good night, Beautiful."

Rest was the last thing she was getting as Maggie lay in bed an hour later. She had taken a long shower, shaved, and moisturized with a scented lotion to get the smell of the lake off of her skin. She had put on her softest nightgown, and the satin fabric was cool against her smooth skin.

She had bandaged the gash on her leg left by the broken glass of the windshield and taken some ibuprofen. A warm cup of tea sat half-empty on her night stand next to the book she couldn't concentrate on reading.

Her mind was full of thoughts and images of her and Jeremy plunging into the lake, of swimming through the raging current of water pouring through the broken window, of the passionate kiss that they shared as the car was sinking. Of him saying "I love you". And of her saying it back.

She stared at the ceiling, wide awake, feeling as if something important had happened. Not just that her life had been threatened, but that her life had changed. Her heart had changed.

In that moment in the car, with the water rising as fast as her panic, something changed, and she knew that she could believe in Jeremy. That she loved him. That she could *trust* him. That she didn't want to go another moment without telling him how she felt.

And now, lying in bed, with sleep eluding her, she didn't feel worried or stressed. She felt happy. She felt loved. She smiled and wrapped her arms around herself. But those were not the arms she wanted to feel.

She didn't have it all figured out, but she knew one thing. She knew where she wanted to be right now, where she *needed* to be. And it wasn't here, in this bed, alone.

Maggie knocked on Jeremy's door, her heart in her throat. She knew it was late, and she prayed he would be glad to see her.

She had no phone to call ahead and warn him that she was coming. Her purse was at the bottom of the lake. Thank goodness she hadn't taken her car keys out on their date.

She was in such a hurry to get to Jeremy, to do something spontaneous for once, that she just grabbed a jacket, threw it on over her nightgown, and jumped in the car. The jacket barely covered her short pajamas and left her legs bare. She had scribbled a quick note saying she went for a drive and would be back soon, and left it on her nightstand just in case anyone came looking for her.

She had no shoes, no driver's license, no wallet. She'd watched her speed as she had driven over, more worried about a cop catching her in a short black satin nightgown with no bra than with no license.

The front door opened, and Jeremy stood there, in a pair of black boxers with a picture of Han Solo and a caption about his light saber on them. His hair was smooshed and stood up in little spikes on the side of his head. He squinted at her through his thick black glasses. He couldn't have looked more nerdy. Or more adorable. And she knew that she loved him.

She gave him a little wave. "Hi."

"Maggie? Is that really you?" He stood back from the door and let her in. The house was dark except for the light from the flames thrown off by the fire that glowed in the fireplace. A pillow and a throw blanket lay haphazardly on the sofa. "I fell asleep on the couch and was just having a dream about you. Am I still dreaming?"

"If you are, then I'm dreaming too. And I don't want to wake up."

He shook his head. "I can't believe you're here."

"Is that okay? That I just showed up? I know it's late."

His face broke into a grin, as if he had just received his favorite gift at Christmas time. "Heck ya, it's okay. It's awesome." He grabbed her and pulled her into a tight hug, lifting her off her feet and planting a kiss on her lips.

She wrapped her legs around his waist and felt his hands slide down her back and cup her bottom under the jacket.

Jeremy pulled back, a mischievous look on his face. "Are you wearing a thong?"

Maggie's face broke into a naughty grin. "Maybe."

"Is it my birthday?"

"It might as well be." She nibbled at the spot she loved, right under his earlobe. "You'll have to unwrap me to get your gift."

He smiled at her, a grin so big it nearly split his face. "Challenge accepted." He carried her into the living room, her legs still tight around his waist, and dumped her onto the sofa. He straddled her and grasped the belt that tied her light jacket shut. "Should I just rip the wrapper off my present to see what's inside? Or should I take it slow and savor the process?"

Maggie looked up at him, the flames of the fire reflected in his brown eyes. She searched his face and all she saw was love and wonder and passion. She felt this was right. This moment was exactly where she was supposed to be, and she knew she loved this man. Her voice was husky and low. "We've got all night. I think you should savor it and take it slow. Really slow."

He pulled the knot loose, and she heard him catch his breath as he carefully opened her jacket and let it fall to the side. Her short black nightgown was pushed up so it barely brushed her thighs. The lacy bodice had shifted as he threw her on the sofa and rode low on her bare breast, scarcely covering her erect nipples, now puckered and hard from want.

He dipped his head, laying a row of gentle kisses along the top edge of her breast and down into the V of her nightgown. His hands brushed softly down her sides, causing her to arch her back against him and let out a low moan of desire.

His lips traveled up her neck, catching her earlobe in his teeth and sending waves of pleasure through her very core. His breath was warm against her throat, and his voice was gruff in her ear. "Maggie, you are so sexy. I want you so bad. I want to touch every inch of you. I want to see every part of you."

The slow patience of his touch ceased as her jacket fell away and the only thing between them was the lace and satin of her nightgown. Maggie lost herself in the feel of his hands as they plunged into her hair. He feasted on her mouth and her neck, tasting her skin as if she were a delicacy to be savored and then devoured.

His hands covered every part of her, sliding and grasping, and she only wanted more. She couldn't get close enough to him. She pushed him back, gasping for breath, then brazenly pulled the nightgown over her head and lay back on the sofa, naked except for the small black lace thong.

She reveled in the look of desire that shone in his eyes as she lay stripped in front of him. She felt as if she had bared not only her body, but her soul to him. Laid herself open to let him in, to trust that he would treasure and not destroy her.

Jeremy leaned above her, consuming her with his eyes. "Baby, you are so beautiful."

A lock of his dark hair fell across his forehead, and Maggie was overwhelmed with how handsome he was and how much she felt for him. She reached up, encircling his neck with her arms and pulled him down, bringing his face to hers and softly kissing his lips.

The feel of their bare skin touching was almost electric, and Maggie felt Jeremy's low moan of passion against her mouth. She gave herself to him, pulling him tighter against her, clutching his muscular back with her hands. She felt his hands slide under her, grasping her bottom, his fingers sliding closer to the center of her desire.

He raised himself above her, only long enough to peel the lacy thong down her legs and shimmy out of his boxers. She missed the heat of his skin on hers and gasped in pleasure as the weight of him settled against her again.

She arched against him, wanting to feel all of him, to give herself to him and to take as well. To take the love that he so freely offered her. To take the gift of his heart and his body. Especially his body. She really wanted to take his body. And right now.

She felt his want. In the way he touched her and in the longing of his kiss. She gasped against his ear as he filled her, and they joined together in a dance of pleasure and desire. A dance that took her soaring, calling out his name, and merging their bodies and souls as they crossed the boundaries of intimacy and ecstasy.

Afterwards, they lay on the floor in front of the fire. The thick, plush rug soft against her bare skin, she pulled the sofa throw down to cover them. Her body was spent. Jeremy lay sprawled next to her, his arm thrown possessively around her waist.

She drew small circles with her fingertips on his muscled biceps. There must be something to this afterglow business, because she felt as if she were glimmering with happiness. A spark welled from inside of her, shining brighter than the golden flames of the fire.

She snuggled against him, burying her face in his neck. She inhaled the expensive aftershave that he wore and knew that his scent now covered her skin.

She spoke into his ear, her voice calm and strong, conveying the emotions she felt, the only emotion strong enough to express the feelings inside of her. "I love you, Jeremy."

Jeremy rolled over and pulled her under him. He swept a lock of hair from her face and kissed her lips with a tenderness that spoke volumes. "I love you too, Maggie."

One soft kiss. One moment of time. But everything had changed. She had changed. She felt different. Lighter. Like a weight had been lifted from her shoulders. Happy.

He lay back and tugged her to him, cradled in his arms. Making one last declaration before drifting off to sleep. "Best birthday present *ever*."

Maggie whipped the eggs into a golden yellow froth and caught herself singing to the radio as she made brunch for the boys. She had snuck back in the house around four in the morning and caught a few hours of sleep.

The rest of the house was sleeping in, so she had taken a bath that morning, soaking her battered body, and found a series of bruises and scrapes resulting from the car crash. Her shoulder was sore from where she had been thrust against the seatbelt during the impact.

She had a couple of bruises that she attributed to falling off the sofa last night with Jeremy and whacking her hip on the coffee table, but those she wore with pride.

Thinking about last night made her smile. She turned the radio up before she poured the eggs into a skillet. Singing along with a top-forty tune, she danced to the refrigerator, wiggling her hips to the beat.

Chad wandered into the kitchen, rubbing his eyes and mumbling about coffee. "Did I hear you singing? What are you so happy about?" He stopped and looked at her. Really looked at her. "Oh. I get it."

Did he? Was he thinking about the fact that he used to make her this happy? If he did, it was so long ago, she could barely remember. In fact, she couldn't recall a time that she had felt such utter bliss.

Chad took a cup from the cupboard. "At least let me get in a cup of coffee before you hit me with the happiness stick. And if you keep singing, I'm afraid some little birds and mice will show up and start sweeping the floor and sewing you a dress."

She took a deep breath, determined not to let Chad's remarks ruin her day. She did feel a bit like Cinderella and that she was in a fairy tale. Only her Prince Charming wore thick-rimmed glasses, spoke computer-ese, and had a *Star Wars* poster in his master bathroom.

Dishing up the scrambled eggs, she put them on the table and turned back to Chad. "Don't rain on my happy parade."

"Well, somebody has to." Chad sipped at the coffee. He always took it black, claiming cream and sugar were for sissies. "Listen, Maggie-May, it's not that I don't like to see you happy. I do." He stepped closer to her and ran his hand lightly up her arm. "In fact, I love seeing you like this. I forgot what a gorgeous smile you have."

What was he playing at? Maggie pulled her arm free and put the pan in the sink. She squirted a stream of dish soap into the skillet. "Maybe that's because you didn't give me much to smile about."

He grimaced. "Ouch. Okay, I deserve that. But this whole experience has changed me. Made me see life from a different perspective."

Yeah. From the perspective of a younger woman's bed. "You brought that experience on yourself, Chad. You're the one who left me."

"I know, and I'm sorry. I don't know if I've ever even told you that. But I truly am sorry for what I did to you. For how I hurt you and the boys."

She looked at him and believed she saw actual pain and regret in his eyes. Geez, one near-death experience and she was giving everyone a second chance. "I appreciate that. But it's over now. I've moved on."

Chad moved a step closer to her, his body almost touching hers. "I know. But I'm not sure that I have. I know that I made a stupid mistake. I will never forgive myself for leaving you and the boys. But these past few weeks, being back in the house, here with my family. Here with you. I feel like I've been granted a second chance."

A second chance? With the kids? Or with her? "I don't know what you mean."

He picked up her hand and ran his thumb along her knuckles. "I think you do. I've been trying to show you how I've changed. How I am trying to be a better man. Being here the past few weeks has shown me what I'm missing out on. Spending time with the kids. And with you."

She didn't know what to say. What exactly was he telling her?

Moving in front her, he slid one hand under her arm and pinned her between his body and the counter behind her. He reached up to touch her hair. "You are so pretty. How did I not see how gorgeous you were? We've known each other since we were kids. I feel like we grew up together, and you were just always there. I guess I took you for granted, stopped *seeing* you."

He brought his hand down to caress her cheek. "I'm seeing you now, Maggie. I see how you've changed. What a strong woman you are. How beautiful you are."

"Beautiful" was Jeremy's word for her. Chad had never told her she was beautiful. He had never talked to her like this at all. Maybe if he had, they could have had a chance. A chance to make it work. She had loved him once. He was her first love, and she would have done anything for him. She had always loved his eyes. She looked into his eyes now and could still see a glimmer of the young man that she married.

Chad leaned into her, his chest brushing against hers. His hand left the counter and gripped her waist. "I know we could make this work. You've changed. I've changed. I know I could be the man you need me to be. Just give me a chance." He dipped his head and pulled her to him, crushing her lips in a passionate kiss.

Give him a chance? What was he talking about? She had given him a chance. More than one. And more importantly, she had given him her heart. Which he had taken, then stomped on, and handed back to her in a Hooters take-out bag.

She pushed him away, wiping her mouth with her fingers. "Chad, stop it! What are you doing?"

He held his ground, his hand still holding her hip. "I'm doing what I should have done a year ago. I'm fighting for you. I want you back. I want *us* back."

"There is no 'us.' You destroyed 'us' when you decided to leave me for another woman."

Chad shook his head. "I know I did. And I said I'm sorry. But I'm back now."

He's back now? And what? That's supposed to make everything okay? Make all the hurt and pain that he caused her just go away. Was he kidding? Who did he think he was? Who did he think *she* was? Showing up on her doorstep, playing dutiful dad and husband for a few weeks and thinking she would just welcome him back with open arms. Forget all that he had done to her?

She pushed against his chest, breaking the connection and taking a step back from him. "Are you serious right now? You *left* me. For another woman. And when that didn't work out, you show up here thinking that I'll just take you back? You think you can unload the dishwasher, go to a few soccer games, make some waffles, and that makes everything all right?"

The time she had spent with Jeremy had taught her that she was worth more than this. She was smart and talented and deserved to be loved for who she really was. Flaws and all. He had taught her that good men did exist. Men who appreciate a woman who thinks for herself, who has opinions, and who isn't afraid to share them.

She had lived under Chad's thumb for too long. Letting him make decisions, even bad ones, without saying a word. Trying to bolster his ego through his role as head of their household. Watching their finances seep away as he purchased new toys and electronics. Well, guess what, buddy? He wasn't in charge anymore.

Chad ran his hand through his hair. "I know it's not going to be easy, but I'm making the effort. You have to see that I'm trying."

"It's too little, too late. You said it yourself. I've changed. I'm not the same woman you were married to. You did that." She pointed at his chest. "You destroyed me. Left me in a simpering pool of heartache and bitterness. But I pulled myself out of that pool. Dried myself off and came out tougher. I had to. Because I didn't have time to wallow in that cesspool of loneliness and anger. I had two kids to take care of. Two boys who still needed to be fed, and driven to school, and to soccer, and to football practice. Who still needed one of their parents to be there for them, to listen and to hug them, and to tell them it wasn't their fault that their dad had left."

Tears were coursing down Maggie's cheeks. She swiped them away with the back of her hand. She didn't care if he saw her cry. He needed to hear this. "What you did was selfish, Chad. You were only thinking of yourself. And you still are. You got tossed out on your ass by your new girlfriend, and suddenly I look a lot better. Suddenly a stable income and spending time as a family holds more appeal than a fake pair of tits."

Chad's face held a look of shock. She knew he wasn't used to hearing her speak to him like this. He must have thought that she would fall back under his spell and back into his arms with some flowery words and the old Chad-charm.

That wasn't happening.

She was finally happy, damnit! It had been a long time since she had felt this good. Since she had woke up in the morning and been excited about her day. And that was because of Jeremy. He had given her back her strength. Helped her to believe in herself. And she had taken her life back. She had finally let go of that bitter front that she wore like a shield of armor.

She had let a man into her life, and he hadn't let her down. He had seen the real Maggie and liked her anyway. And she let herself trust again. Opened her heart and let herself feel.

She drew on that strength now. She wrenched every ounce of courage from deep inside of her. She lifted her chin in steely resolve. "I think it's time for you to find your own place. For real. I need you to move out."

Chad's eyes widened, and he held up his hands. "Hold on there, Maggie. You can't mean it. Things have been good since I've been here. We haven't been fighting. I've been spending time with the boys. Look, we can take it slow. There's no need to rush things. All I'm asking is for you to think about it."

Maggie shook her head. "There's nothing to think about. I appreciate that you're spending time with the boys, and I hope that doesn't change. They need you in their lives. But I don't. I've moved on and found someone else. And I'm actually happy."

The look of desperation on Chad's face turned to a sneer. "Is that what this is really about? Some nerdy rich guy who takes you out to dinner and pays you a few compliments? He throws around some money, and you drop your panties for him, and now all of a sudden you're happy?"

Maggie gulped, swallowing against the burn of the bile and anger rising in her throat. This was the Chad she knew. The real Chad. The one who didn't get his way and fought back with poison and venom. "It's over, Chad. We're not getting back together."

"Because some guy pays attention to you? You don't even know him. You finally get some and now you're confusing afterglow with happiness."

"We're done here. Pack up your stuff. Tell the boys goodbye, then I want you to leave."

"You're making a mistake, Maggie. If I leave, I'm not coming back."

His threats and guilt had no power over her. She didn't need him. She was strong enough now to stand her ground. "That's fine."

The anger poured from him, almost visible in waves of red surrounding the air around him. "You're gonna regret this. You're throwing away a chance at having our lives back for a guy who could be a murderer."

She watched his temper rise. This was all too familiar. But now she was different. As his anger grew, hers subsided. She refused to take his bait, and felt herself become calmer. More focused. "You don't get it, Chad. I *have* my life back. Regardless if Jeremy is in it or not. This is *my* life now. And I'm proud of it. I've been taking care of myself and the boys and doing a great job. I don't need you anymore. You broke my heart, but now I'm over it. I'm over you."

She turned away and gasped as she saw Drew standing in the doorway of the kitchen. His eyes glistened with tears. She wondered how much he had heard.

He took two steps and pulled her into his arms, crushing her in a bear hug. His voice was hoarse with emotion. "I love you, Mom. I'm proud of you."

When had she blinked and her son had turned into a man? Thank goodness he understood. She squeezed him back, proud of *both* of them.

Drew looked at his father, his voice now low and controlled. "I love you too, Dad, and I hope we can hang out some before I leave for college. But for now, how about I help you pack?"

Maggie sat on her back deck the next day and sipped a cup of coffee, her favorite vanilla creamer swirled in to turn the black brew to a creamy caramel color. She loved Sunday mornings, getting up early and enjoying the peace of the house before the boys got up and requested breakfast.

Her backyard was an oasis, her deck furniture covered in shades of blue and green fabric, soft pillows tucked in the corners. The boys had helped her string twinkle lights along the railing last summer and various candles and outdoor lanterns sat on end tables and the deck rails. She had planted a truckload of annuals earlier that spring, and her flower gardens exploded with colorful pansies, snapdragons, and petunias.

She sighed as she leaned back into the cushions. The morning air was cool, and she could almost smell a hint of autumn in the air. Time for a change.

She felt as if her very existence was changing. Drew was leaving for college. She had stood up to Chad and kicked him out. And she was in love.

She couldn't help but smile as she thought of Jeremy and the night they had spent together. On the sofa, in front of the fireplace, on the floor. A blush accompanied her smile as she felt her cheeks warm thinking about how brazen she had been with him. And how much fun it had been.

She felt like a new chapter in her life was starting. An exciting chapter. She could do change. Right now, she felt like she could do just about anything.

A huge weight felt lifted from her shoulders. A five foot ten grumbling ex-husband weight. Chad was not happy about it, but he had packed his things up and moved out the night before. A friend of his had a converted garage apartment and offered to let Chad stay there in exchange for helping him put an addition on his house. Seemed like Chad could have moved out weeks ago. But at least he was gone now. Maggie could move on.

Move on to the next adventure in her life. And her love life. Now if she could just prove that her nerdy new boyfriend was innocent of murder, she would really be happy.

The doorbell rang. Her heart leapt as she hoped it was that nerdy new boyfriend now. She would love to share her Sunday morning ritual in the backyard with him.

She opened the front door. Not her cute new boyfriend. Still cute, just not her boyfriend. Officer McCarthy stood on her doorstep wearing a handsome grin and holding her purse.

"Hey Mac." She pulled the door wider and gestured for him to come in. "Nice purse. It matches your shoes."

"Thanks. I try to stick with basic black."

She laughed. "How in the world did you get my purse?"

He stepped into the living room and set her purse on the coffee table. He opened it and pulled out a bag of rice, the tip of her cell phone poking out of the top of the bag. "We don't see a lot of this kind of excitement around here. The divers and the wrecking crew were there bright and early yesterday and we spent most of the day pulling your boyfriend's SUV out of the lake. We recovered your purse and a few tools that were still in the car, but that's about it."

"I can't believe you got my purse out. And my phone. I haven't had a lot of luck with phones lately." She gestured to the bag on the table. "What's with the rice?"

"They say if your phone gets wet or dropped in water, that you can stick it in a bag of rice. It absorbs the moisture from the phone, then it works again. I had a bag of rice at home so I threw your phone in there last night. It should be dry by now. No guarantees that it will work, but you can pull it out and try it."

Maggie tugged her phone out of the rice and put it back together. She turned it on and waited for it to power up. "Do you know anything more about who did this?"

"Nah. There's a big scrape on the driver's side of the car where he must have rammed into you and a dent in the back bumper, but that's about all we've got. I wish you could have gotten a look at them or a license plate number."

"Me too. Believe me, I'm as anxious as you are to find out who's behind all this. Do you think we're still in danger?" At Maggie's question, her phone chirped and buzzed several times as texts and missed calls appeared on the screen. What do you know? The rice worked. She glanced at the display, noting a message from a blocked number.

"Oh no. Mac, look at this." She held her phone up, and he pressed against her side, leaning in to see the tiny screen. The message freaked her out, but not enough for her to ignore the hard muscles of his body next to hers or the musky aftershave that he wore. She was still a woman.

Mac read the message aloud: *I told you to leave it alone. Next time you'll get more than a big drink of water.* He looked questioningly at Maggie. "What are they talking about? What did you do?"

Maggie shrugged. "Nothing. We did all those Google searches, but no one could have known about that. I did tell Jeremy."

"Do you really trust this guy?" Mac looked at her, as if searching her eyes for the truth. "Because it sure seems to me like there's more going on than meets the eye."

She nodded. "I do trust him. I really don't believe that he could kill someone. He did tell me he had a staff meeting yesterday and told his employees that the police were getting closer to arresting someone. He was trying to flush out the killer."

"What? Idiot. Why would he do that?"

"He saw it on *Law & Order*, and it worked."

"Well, I saw a knife that cut through a pop can on TV and it worked, but when I got it home, it was a piece of junk. You can't always believe what you see on television."

"He was trying to help."

Mac grunted. "Maybe he should form a club with your friend, Edna. The Amateur Detective/Crime Show Watchers Club."

Maggie laughed, despite the insult to both her friend and her boyfriend. "They have good intentions."

"Yeah, well, good intentions can get somebody hurt." He touched the scraped side of her arm where she had grazed it against the broken edges of the windshield.

She shivered from the light touch of his hand and the memory of her terrifying ordeal. "So, what should we do? Just sit around and wait for them to send more threats or do something worse than try to run us off the road? They could have actually killed one or both of us that night."

"I am well aware of that fact, Maggie. And I don't want anything to happen to you." He winked at her. She wasn't sure if he was flirting or just trying to lighten the situation. "I've grown quite fond of you."

Quite fond of her? He sounded like a lawman out of an old western. But usually those lawmen were pretty hot, so maybe she should try a different train of thought.

"I think you're nice too." *Oh, my gosh.* Who had the lame line now? She looked around for anything to save her from the direction of this conversation. "Thanks for bringing over my purse. You didn't have to go to the trouble. That was really thoughtful. I appreciate it." *Just stop talking. Now.*

"Plus, it gave me a chance to check on you and make sure you were all right."

She took a deep breath. "I'm fine. But I would be a lot better if you catch the real killer, and I stop getting these terrible texts."

Several hours later, the doorbell rang again and Maggie hollered, "Come in!"

Her house felt like Grand Central Station lately. She sat at her office desk, trying and failing to concentrate on work. She had brought some case files home, but each time she tried to concentrate on reading one, her thoughts drifted to Jeremy. To the way he touched her and called her Beautiful. Or to the way he saved her from their terrifying ordeal.

Sunny poked her head in the office door. "Hey, it's me. And Jake's here too." Jake leaned over Sunny's blond head and waved.

Maggie motioned them in, turning her office chair to face them as they sat on the plaid loveseat in her office. "I told you I was okay. You didn't need to check on me."

Sunny leaned forward and took her hand. "I'm your friend. That's what friends do." She smiled, but Maggie could tell her whole heart wasn't in it. She was holding something back.

"And…what else do friends do?"

Sunny sighed. "Deliver bad news in person, I guess. Jake wanted to see that most recent text message, and he also had something to show you."

A new wave of fear slammed into Maggie. She knew she didn't want to see anything Jake had to show her. From Sunny's expression, she knew it was bad and that it must be about Jeremy.

She wanted to scream. To stand up and tell them to leave. To get out of her house. To just let her have *one day* to enjoy being happy. One freaking day.

But she didn't. She didn't stand up, and she didn't scream or tell them to leave. She took a deep breath and closed her eyes, bracing herself for the blow. "Go ahead. Tell me."

Jake pulled a folded sheaf of papers from his hand. "Finney and I have been tracing all the electronic correspondence of Jeremy's company. We found some emails that accuse Jim of selling digital secrets to SkyVision and outright threaten him with bodily harm if he doesn't quit. One says that he'll be sorry and another hints that his life could be in danger if he doesn't stop dealing with SkyVision and return the codes that he stole. "

Maggie let out the breath she was holding. This wasn't so bad. In fact, it was good news. "That's great. If we can show evidence of an actual death threat to the police, then that should point us to the killer."

Jake looked at the floor. "Yeah. That's the problem. The emails are from Jeremy."

For the second time in two days, Maggie raced to Jeremy's house. But this time, she was wearing a bra. She was fully clothed, and the stack of emails lay in the seat next to her.

This time, she was going straight to the source. She was going to face Jeremy and ask him to explain these messages. No fooling around, no spending a day spying on him while she followed him all over a comic book convention. She had the proof in her hands and she was determined to get answers.

She pulled up in front of Jeremy's house and noticed a small red sports car in the driveway. Jeremy had told her he was meeting some guys to play basketball. One of them must have brought him home, since Jeremy's car was currently drying out from its recent swim in the lake.

It might be a little more awkward to confront Jeremy in front of his friend, but oh well. She needed to know the truth.

Reaching for the doorbell, Maggie noticed the front door was open an inch, so she gently pushed against it. The door swung wide open, as if beckoning her to come inside. She poked her head in the door, but the house seemed empty. The living room was neatly picked up, and she flashed on the memory of her and Jeremy, naked on the rug in front of the fireplace.

If she was welcome to get naked in the living room, she guessed she could come in without knocking first. Maybe the guys were in the backyard, cooling off in the pool after their game. She stepped into the house and was met with silence.

Peeking into the kitchen, she could see the backyard through the sliding glass door. The swimming pool glittered in the late-afternoon sun, but there were no sweaty basketball-playing men immersed in it.

She could see the dog run. Chewie sat behind the fence, one paw raised and rested against the chain link. As if he recognized her, the dog gave a bark of greeting. If Jeremy was home, why hadn't he let the dog inside?

Maybe this wasn't such a good idea. She could go home, try calling first. A sound from above her head caused her to jump. She laughed at herself. This was silly. She was here. And she wanted answers.

She climbed the steps, calling out Jeremy's name. "Hello. Anybody home?"

Her heart was racing as she progressed up the stairs. The threatening text message came to mind, and an ominous feeling of dread filled her. What if the killer had come here to take care of Jeremy? What if she was too late? Or worse, what if the killer was still in the house?

She looked around for a weapon to arm herself with. All she carried was her purse—a new one she had in the closet, not the soggy one that Mac had dropped off this morning—and a handful of emails. Was she going to defend herself by threatening them with paper cuts?

A heavy iron statue of an elephant sat on a table on the landing with a stack of antique books leaning against it. Maggie hefted the elephant against her shoulder. At best, she could whack someone on the head with it. At the very least, she could throw it at someone.

She slowly approached Jeremy's bedroom, her footsteps muffled by the thick carpet. His door was partially open, and she could hear the shower running in the master bathroom. As she got closer, she heard him singing, the lyrics to an old Eagles song carrying over the sound of the shower.

She let out her breath. Oh, brother. She had freaked out for nothing. He was just in the shower. She heard the water turn off, and his singing stopped.

Maybe that wasn't a friend's car. Maybe he had already gotten a rental. Maggie pushed open the door of the bedroom.

Jeremy and his mom had decorated his house, and Maggie particularly liked what they had done in the master bedroom. She loved the masculine feel of the gold and deep reds and the heavy dark wood of the furniture. But the one decorative feature that she wasn't expecting in the room was the naked blonde lying seductively in Jeremy's bed.

Clad only in a towel and shaking his wet head, Jeremy stepped out of the bathroom and froze. He looked at Maggie, then at Charlotte lying in his bed and then back at Maggie again, his head doing a confused ping-pong action between the two women. "What are you doing here? And what are you doing with that elephant?"

The statue slipped from Maggie's hands and hit the floor with a heavy thud. The stack of emails floated to the floor like a white flurry of snowflakes. The sight of Jeremy coming out of the shower to a naked younger woman in his bed was more than she could bear. She choked on a sob and backed out of the room, turning and fleeing down the stairs. She heard Jeremy call her name, but she was out the door and running for her car.

She threw the car in gear and peeled out. She saw Jeremy standing in his front yard, the white towel around his waist, waving at her, but she couldn't get out of there fast enough. Screw it if she got a ticket. She needed to get as far away from him as fast as possible.

How could she have let herself get sucked into his lies? He was one more man who had chosen a younger woman over her. When would she learn? How had she let her guard down? Let herself trust again? Somehow this betrayal felt worse than it had with Chad, because she should have known better. She let herself get tricked into believing that Jeremy cared for her. Loved her.

She should have known. The man created video games for a living. She must have been just another game to him. The ultimate game of cat and mouse. He was the predator, and she was the prey.

And now she had been caught. And slain. Her heart lay open and bleeding, torn to shreds by the man she thought she loved.

Her cell phone began to ring in her purse, and she threw the bag to the floor of the car. She turned the radio up full blast and ignored the incessant ringing. Her heart-wrenching sobs were drowned out by the loud music as she beat the steering wheel in frustration.

How could he have done this to her? How could she have fallen for his lies? Never again would she let herself trust. Never again would she allow herself to be hurt like this. To bear the physical pain of loss and betrayal. The anguish in her chest threatened to choke her, and the sorrow lay like a heavy brick in her stomach. She would never give another man a chance to hurt her like this. She would never suffer this pain again. Never again.

Maggie slogged through the next week, wading through her days as if they were filled with molasses. She buried herself in her work, ignoring calls and visits from her friends. And from Jeremy.

She had told the kids that she needed time to be alone and not to bother her. And if anyone stopped by, they were instructed to tell them to go away.

Jeremy had tried repeatedly to call her. She let all of his calls go to voicemail and deleted the messages without listening to them. She had heard enough lies.

He had come to the house several times and she told her family not to answer the door. The boys had been gone the last time he had come by and Maggie had curled into the corner of the sofa, her arms wrapped around her knees, sobbing as she listened to him pound on the door and call her name. She had pulled herself into a tight ball of despair, rocking against the sofa cushion, as she waited for him to give up and walk away.

Thank goodness Chad had moved out. That would have been one more reminder of how gullible she had been. Believing in another man and giving him the chance to rip her heart out.

A knock on her office door had her looking up from the case files she was working on. What the heck was he doing here? "Hey, Mac."

The police officer stood in her doorway, his expression grim. "Hey, Maggie. Sorry to bother you at work."

Maggie closed the file. A feeling of dread filled her as she waited for the next piece of news that Mac was here to share. "It's okay. You don't typically show up bearing good news."

"I know. And I'm afraid today is no exception."

She sighed and gestured to the chairs in front of her desk. "Have a seat. I'm already having a shitty week, so you probably can't make it worse." *Oh, please, do not make it worse.*

Mac sat on the chair, his tall body filling the seat. He leaned forward, his forearms resting on his muscular thighs.

Why was she even looking at his muscles? She had sworn off men. A wave of fresh pain shot through her as she thought of Jeremy and the image of Charlotte wrapped in the crisp sheets of his bed. The same sheets that Jeremy had laid her back against and made love to her on.

How could she move on? Anger and bitterness swirled inside of her, mixed with hurt and confusion as to how he could have done this to her. How he could have fooled her like this.

And one thing Maggie Hayes knew: she hated being made a fool of. She had to put Jeremy behind her. Stop obsessing about him and how he had hurt her.

She turned her attention back to Mr. Cute Cop and tried to focus on his news and not how well he filled out his uniform. Might as well get the bad news out of the way. Rip it off like a Band-Aid. "So, what do you know?"

Mac shook his head. "I know that it stinks that I'm the one who has to tell you these things. I hate causing you pain. I would much rather be the guy that makes you smile."

Was he actually flirting with her? She knew there was some attraction between them, but it sounded like a few compliments weren't going to be enough to soften the blow of what was coming. "Just tell me. What's going on?"

The policeman sighed. "Some new evidence has come to light that puts Jeremy at the scene of the crime."

"What kind of evidence?"

"Video showing him going into the office."

"Of course there is video of him going into his office. He works there. He *has* to go there."

"The video is time-stamped with the date and time. It shows Jeremy in the office early on the morning of the murder. He claims he left on Friday night and didn't return to the office until we called him down on Saturday."

Another lie. It seemed Jeremy was not the man she thought he was at all. "How are you just figuring this out now? Why haven't you looked at the video before?"

"We did. That's why this was a little odd. One of Jeremy's employees brought the video to us. He claims he had it but didn't want to get Jeremy in trouble."

Maggie tapped the files in front of her with a pen. "Who is this employee who just happened to be withholding evidence?" She tried to keep the sneer out of her voice, but she imagined a tearful Charlotte showing up at the police station, holding the evidence against her substantial bosom. The same ones that rested against Jeremy's sheets.

Mac pulled a notepad from his pocket and flipped to an ear-marked page. "It was that squirrely guy. Leonard."

"Leonard?" Why would Leonard give incriminating evidence to the police?

"Yeah. He came in this morning and said he had something to show us. I guess the guy is really paranoid and has some sort of security device on his desktop at work that records movement around his desk. He claims it took him awhile to remember and when he ran back through the recording, it was a little blurred so he wasn't sure if it was Jeremy. I guess he designed some type of image-sharpening software and ran the recording through it, and it very clearly shows Jeremy walking by his desk."

Maggie's heart sank. "Are you sure it was him?"

Mac nodded. "You can see his dark hair and his face, and evidently he was wearing some custom-made jacket that's easily recognizable in the video. I'm sorry, Maggie."

As mad as she was at him for cheating on her, she still never believed he was capable of hurting anyone.

Although he had hurt her. She felt a pain inside of her, as if her heart were being ripped in half. A lone tear rolled down her cheek.

"Ah, come on now. Don't do that." Mac stood up and came around the desk. He pulled Maggie from her chair and into his arms. "I can't stand to see you cry."

Something about the way he held her gently against his shoulder and caressed her hair completely did Maggie in. The floodgates loosened, and she cried against his shoulder. Big, soul-shaking sobs of pain. Her hands came around his waist, and she gripped his crisp uniform shirt in her hands. "I can't believe this is happening."

"I know. This one surprised me too. I thought the guy was all right." He pulled her head back, wiping her tears away with his thumb. "But it's unacceptable that he hurt you and made you cry."

Maggie nodded and wiped at his shoulder. "Thanks, Mac. Sorry I got tears on your shoulder."

"I don't mind." Mac looked down at her, a serious look on his face. His arms were still wrapped around her and he pulled her a little tighter against him. "Maggie, I know this isn't the best timing, but it's no secret that I'm interested in you."

Uh oh. Another man interested in her was not what she needed right now. She needed her dog and some tea and a good book and warm socks. And macaroni and cheese. She did not need a sexy cop looking at her with desire in his eyes. Especially one that rode a motorcycle and looked amazing in jeans and a leather jacket.

Mac dipped his head and softly kissed her.

Maggie pulled back, shaking her head. "I'm sorry, Mac. I'm not ready."

He sighed. "No, I'm the one who's sorry. I shouldn't have done that. I've just been thinking about you, and you look so beautiful. I was out of line."

She noticed he hadn't let go of her yet, though. She reached up and laid a hand against his cheek. He was a good guy and she didn't want to hurt him. "It's okay. I'm just reeling from the break-up with Jeremy and can't even think about anyone else right now. I *am* attracted to you." She smiled up at him, trying for a joke to lighten the mood. "I mean, who wouldn't be? Look at these muscles."

He laughed as she playfully squeezed his biceps. He hugged her tight against him for a second, then let her go. "Well, you know how to find me when you're ready."

"Thank you," she whispered softly.

He headed for the door. "I'll let you know if I hear anything more on the case."

"Hey, Mac." Maggie called to him, and he turned back to her. Though her heart was still reeling from the pain of Jeremy's betrayal, she knew what it was like to put yourself out there and get rejected. Mac had only been good to her and she didn't want him to walk out the door on a bad note. "Just so you know, you're a pretty great kisser."

A sexy grin crossed his face. "Thanks. But I am a detective. I know you're just giving me one last boost to my ego." He shook his head. "Like it's not bad enough that I lose out to a total nerd. I mean, seriously, what grown man wears an emblem of his favorite video game on his jacket? Who even knows what Warcraft World is anyway?"

"*World of Warcraft.*" She absently corrected him, feeling another wave of sadness that she wouldn't be able to play the online game with her favorite player anymore. One more loss in her life. She waved at Mac. "See you later."

"Take care, Maggie. And remember, I'm here if you need me." He pulled her office door shut behind him.

She sank into her chair and opened a file. She took a sip of cold coffee from the cup on her desk and tried to concentrate on the case in front of her.

Her mind swirled with images of Jeremy and how they met. How they had known each other's alter egos in their favorite online game and the time they had actually played together before meeting in person.

Since they had started dating, they'd had so much fun together, spending hours playing online, staying up too late, and flirting between their characters in the chat boxes. Geez, maybe she was as nerdy as he was.

Something niggled at the edge of her mind as she read the same paragraph in the file for the third time. Something Mac had said. She took another sip of coffee and reached for the phone, ready to call her assistant to get her a fresh cup.

Holy crap! She froze, her hand in midair, halfway to the phone. Mac had said that Leonard identified Jeremy by his custom-made jacket and had asked what kind of man wears a video game emblem on his coat. An emblem of *World of Warcraft.*

The kind of man who designs video games for a living and lets his girlfriend borrow his favorite jacket when they are out on a date and she's cold. The same jacket that had been hanging in her closet for weeks! There was no way that Jeremy walked into his office the morning of the murder wearing that coat. She had taken his jacket the week before the murder, and she still had it at her house.

So, if the video showed Jeremy at his office with a time stamp of Saturday morning, that must mean the recording was a fake! Why would Leonard present a fake recording that would incriminate Jeremy to the police?

Maggie could only think of one reason. That Leonard had something to do with Jim's murder and was trying to frame Jeremy.

She had to tell him. She grabbed the phone and dialed Jeremy's number. It rang several times then went to voicemail. She slammed the phone down and reached for her purse. Jeremy's office was only a few blocks from hers. She could be there in five minutes. She had to warn him about what Leonard was up to.

As she raced for her car, her cell phone rang. Unlocking the car door, she slid in and pulled the phone from her purse. She tucked the phone under her ear and started the engine. "Hello."

"Hey, Maggie. It's Sunny. I'm so glad you answered your phone. Don't hang up."

"Oh, Sunny. I'm sorry." Maggie felt bad that she had ignored her friend's attempts at offering support. "I won't hang up. I'm doing better now."

"Good. We can get into all that 'ignore Cassie and Sunny's calls' business later. And we *will* talk about it later. But for now, I had to tell you that I just talked to Jake. He told me he and Finn have been going through all of Jeremy's emails, and they've discovered that his email account was hacked."

"So what? Like, he just won the Canadian lottery or a princess in Nigeria needs his help and if he just sends her a little money now, she'll repay him in gold and treasure later?"

"Oh, my gosh. Why are you always so cynical?"

Maggie turned out of the parking lot, her attention on getting to Jeremy's office, not discussing a Nigerian scam on his email. "I'm not cynical. I'm a realist."

"A frustrating realist! Would you just listen? The emails that were hacked were the ones that were sent to Jim. The ones that threatened him. Finn figured out that they came from a different IP address and were hacked into Jeremy's account to make it look like he sent them."

"Who would do that?"

"Obviously, someone wanted to set Jeremy up. To make it look like he threatened Jim. Now, I don't have all of Edna's crime-show-watching experience, but I'm pretty sure the only one that would benefit would be the actual murderer."

Maggie was overcome with a feeling of happiness. One more piece of the puzzle showing that Jeremy was innocent. And if he was innocent of these other things, maybe he hadn't really slept with Charlotte. Although a naked blonde in his bed was a pretty big puzzle piece to ignore.

Maggie turned the corner into the parking garage of Jeremy's office. "That's not the only time someone tried to make Jeremy look guilty." She quickly explained about Mac's visit and the bogus recording putting Jeremy at the crime scene. "I'm headed to Jeremy's office right now to let him know what's going on."

"It sounds like the real murderer keeps trying to frame Jeremy. And he keeps upping his game. If this Leonard guy is really the one that's responsible, he could be at the office now. Working with Jeremy. What if he sees you come in?"

"So what? I've visited Jeremy's office before."

"I think you should wait. Call the police and have Mac go in with you."

Maggie hadn't told her the part about Mac kissing her. "All we have is circumstantial evidence. I just want to talk to Jeremy. Tell him what we found out. I'm not ready to have the SWAT team raid the place." Maggie pulled into a parking spot and turned off the engine. "Look, Sunny, I just parked. I'll call you after I talk to Jeremy, all right?"

"All right. I guess. But please be careful."

Maggie hung up her phone and dropped it in her purse. She strode across the parking garage, anxious to get to Jeremy. But now Sunny's warning had her spooked. What if someone was spying on her? The same person who had sent her those texts. And tried to run them off the road.

She slowed her pace, trying to appear normal. Keeping a watchful eye for anything out of the ordinary, she drew up short as she walked past a familiar car. It was the dark burgundy Mercury Marquis that Edna had seen at Comic Con. She hadn't paid that much attention to the license plate, but how many cars could there be like this? And in Jeremy's office parking lot?

She stepped along the side of the car and nonchalantly peeked through the car window. The car was empty, so she leaned in to see if she could see anything on the seats.

"Psst! Psst! Maggie."

Maggie jumped and let out a little shriek as she heard someone whispering her name. Her hand flew to her rapidly beating heart as she looked around the parking structure.

The concrete levels kept out the majority of the mid-afternoon sun, and Maggie realized that she was not alone in the otherwise deserted garage. She reached in her purse for the mace that Edna had bought each of the book club members for Christmas the year before and hoped she remembered how to use it. Then prayed she wouldn't have to.

"Psst! Over here!"

Maggie looked across to the cement pillar reading "Parking Level 1A" and groaned as she saw a familiar silver-haired woman crouched beside a minivan and waving her over. Speak of the mace-gifting devil herself. "Edna! You scared me to death. What are you doing?"

"Shhh! I'm on a stake-out."

"Edna, get over here."

The older woman poked her head from between the rows of parked cars. She looked both ways then duck-walked across the parking garage. She wore dark sunglasses and a khaki trench coat. The tails of the coat dragged on the ground as Edna waddled over. She made it to the rear of the Mercury Marquis and pushed herself up with a groan. "The old knees aren't what they used to be."

"Aren't what they used to be? Have you had a lot of experience waddling across cement parking lots?"

Edna winked at her as she rubbed her sore knees. "I've had a lot of experience doing just about everything."

Maggie rolled her eyes. "What are you doing here?"

"I told you that I recognized this car. I couldn't get anyone to trace that license plate for me, so I've just been keeping my eye out for it. You know I do Zumba across the street, and I saw it here this afternoon, so I decided to scope it out."

"And you just happened to have a Sherlock Holmes wannabe trench coat in your car?" Maggie asked, almost surprised that she wasn't wearing a deerstalker cap and smoking a pipe.

"I like to be prepared."

"Well, what have you seen?"

Edna counted on her fingertips. "Four business men in suits walked by, a woman carrying a baby in one of those car seat thingies, and I'm pretty sure I saw a couple of thugs making a drug deal. Oh, and I saw a couple sneak out to that blue car over there and crawl in the back seat and make out for a bit."

"Geez. How long have you been here?"

The older woman shrugged. "I don't know. An hour or so. Not long enough to see anyone come out and get in this baby, though." Edna tapped the trunk of the Mercury Marquis.

Both women grabbed for each other in fright as something inside the trunk tapped back.

"Holy poop! I think I just had a heart attack." Edna looked down the front of her shirt as if her heart might have actually fallen out of her chest. "What the heck was that?"

"I don't know, but it scared the crap out of me." Maggie tapped on the trunk again. A muffled banging sound answered. Maggie's eyes widened. "There's someone in there."

"Yeah, there is. And you're about to join her."

Maggie and Edna grabbed for each other again as they heard the male voice behind them. They turned and gasped in unison as they stared into the barrel of a gun.

Leonard stood behind them, his hand shaking as he held the gun pointed at them. He passed a set of keys to Maggie and gestured to the trunk. "Open it."

Maggie took the keys and popped the trunk, terrified at what would be inside. Expecting a bloody and mangled body, she was surprised to see only a lumpy shape wrapped in an old army blanket. A shock of blond hair poked out the end of the blanket, and Maggie was pretty sure whose lumpy shape was now wiggling around and making muffled noises. "You don't have to do this. We can just pretend this never happened. We'll walk away and won't say a word to anyone."

Leonard's mouth took on an ugly sneer. "Do you think I'm an idiot? I can't let you walk away now. You've seen too much. I warned you to keep your nose out of it, but you wouldn't listen. Now you'll have to pay."

So, the threatening texts were from Leonard. One mystery solved. But Maggie didn't want to create another one. The Case of the Missing Old Lady and Her Lawyer Friend. An unfortunately-timed giggle threatened to escape from Maggie's throat and she swallowed it down. Why did she always want to laugh at the worst times? The last thing she wanted was for Leonard to think she was laughing at him.

She looked over at Edna, who was discreetly trying to pull something from her bag. Maggie's heart leapt to her throat as watched the older woman pull a large silver revolver from her bag.

Edna pointed the gun at Leonard. "Who's gonna pay now, sucka?"

Without warning, Leonard's arm shot out and knocked the gun from Edna's hand. It hit the cement with a loud thud, and Maggie thought it lucky that the thing didn't go off.

Edna huffed and snarled at their assailant. "Now what'd you do that for? That was my best gun."

Ignoring her, Leonard held out his empty hand. "Give me your bags."

Edna passed over her huge tote bag, and Maggie handed him her slim black purse.

He looped them over his arm and motioned for more. "Hand over your cell phones."

Maggie pointed at his arm. "Mine's in my bag."

Leonard gave her a questioning look. "I'll check when I get in the car. You better not be lying to me." He pointed the gun at Edna. "How about you. Where's your cell phone?"

"What cell phone? I'm eighty-two years old. I still have a rotary phone and a dial-up modem. I have no use for those new-fangled toys."

Leonard narrowed his eyes at her, as if he were not sure whether to believe her. "Well, you had a gun."

Edna laughed. "Cowboys and Indians had guns." She lifted her arms and wiggled her hips suggestively. "Do you want to search me?"

Leonard recoiled in horror. "No, absolutely not." He waved the gun at Maggie. "Get in the trunk."

Maggie climbed in and lay against the lumpy shape. The lump grunted when Maggie *accidentally* kicked it in the shin.

Leonard pointed at Edna. "Now you."

Edna smiled sweetly. "I don't think there's enough room for me in there. Besides, I'm actually quite claustrophobic and tend to get a little car-sick. How about I just ride up front with you?"

Leonard stared at her in disbelief. The veins in his neck bulged as he clenched the muscles in his jaw. "Lady, get in the trunk. Now."

"Fine. It was just a suggestion. You don't have to get all touchy about it." Edna awkwardly climbed into the trunk, falling into Maggie before turning and spooning against her as she squeezed into the leftover space. She looked up at Leonard as he reached to close the trunk. "It's a little tight in here, but it's a nice trunk. You've kept this car in great condition. You know, we used to have a Mercury Marquis."

Leonard rolled his eyes and leaned into the trunk. "I don't care what you used to have. We're gonna go for a little ride now. And just so you know, lady, it is a nice car, and if you throw up in it, I *will* shoot you." He slammed the trunk, leaving the women in the dark.

Maggie poked at Edna. "What are you thinking? Chatting him up about how nice his car is? I was waiting for you to invite him over for tea."

"I was building rapport. Classic first step in hostage negotiations. Maggie, you really should watch more television."

"Yeah, I'll get right on that." Maggie grunted as the women shifted against each other with the motion of the car. She could tell Leonard had reversed and was now pulling out of the parking garage. She tried to focus on the turns they were making, but was quickly disoriented and lost track.

Edna shifted. "Did you get the phone?"

"What phone?"

"My cell phone. I dropped it in your lap when I fell against you. Do you think I am so clumsy that I can't crawl into a trunk?"

"Where was your phone? You told Leonard you didn't have it."

"I didn't want him to know I had it. I always keep it in my bra. I knew he wouldn't really frisk me. I keep tons of stuff in my bra. It's not doing much of anything else. I usually use it like a second purse. I think I have a package of trail mix in there if you're hungry."

"Eww. No thanks, I'm good." Maggie felt around by her stomach and found the phone. She pushed a button and laughed as the display lit up the trunk. She leaned against her friend in a one-armed hug. "Edna, you are a true gem. I love you."

"As much as I appreciate that, quit dry-humping me and call 911."

Maggie's elbow pushed back as she tried to reach the keypad of the phone. The lump wriggled behind her. "I think Charlotte is in the trunk with us. What should I do?"

"Why hasn't she said anything?"

"She's probably gagged." Maggie did not want to admit the perverse pleasure she took in making that statement.

"Can you reach her?"

Maggie twisted around and pulled at the blanket covering the lump. She hit a button on the phone and turned the lit display toward the lump. A wave of terror filled her as she had the sudden thought that this might not be Charlotte, and they could be stuck in the trunk with a stranger. She pointed the phone at the shape and pulled the blanket down, releasing her breath in relief as she recognized the head of blond hair.

Charlotte's eyes were wide above the strip of duct tape that covered her mouth. Maggie wiggled against her, trying to maneuver her arm up to get a hold of the tape. As much disdain as she had for this woman, she also felt compassion for how afraid Charlotte must have been, bound and gagged and trapped in the dark, confined space of the trunk.

Maggie's fingers closed on the corner of the tape. "Get ready. I'm going to yank, and this is probably gonna hurt." She tugged at the tape, pulling it free in one motion.

Charlotte took in huge gulps of air, sobbing as she gasped. "Oh, my gosh. Thank you so much. I've been in this trunk since Leonard went to work this morning."

Maggie twisted back around, intent on trying to dial the three digits on the phone. She touched 911 and then pushed the phone up to her ear, silently praising God when the operator answered the phone.

"911. What is your emergency?"

"We're trapped in the trunk of a car. My name is Maggie Hayes, and I am in trunk of a burgundy Mercury Marquis with Edna Allen and Charlotte Foster."

"Please calm down and speak slowly, ma'am. Did you say there are three of you trapped in the trunk of a car?"

"Yes, we need help."

"Ma'am, this line is for serious emergencies. You can get in a lot of trouble for pranking the 911 line."

"I'm not joking around! Is Officer McCarthy there? Could I please speak to him? This is a serious emergency."

The operator hesitated, then spoke in an annoyed tone. "All right. I'll patch you through to Officer McCarthy's cell phone. But if you really know him, just call him directly next time and keep the emergency line clear."

The lyrical notes of hold music filled Maggie's ear as she sighed in frustration. "She doesn't believe we have an emergency. She thinks I'm just interested in Mac."

Charlotte cried softly behind her. Maggie tilted her head back. "Don't worry, Charlotte. We know a cop. He's gonna help us get out of here."

Charlotte gasped for breath. "I know. That's why I'm crying. I feel terrible. I have been thinking awful things about you and now here you are, trying to help me. You're nothing like what I expected. I thought you would be a snooty, sarcastic bitch."

"She is," Edna said. "You just happened to catch her on a good day."

Maggie poked at Edna with her free hand. "Thanks a lot." She put the phone on speaker so she could hear if Mac came on the line, then tilted it to shine around the trunk. "Why don't you make yourself useful and try to find something to smash the brake-light reflectors. Feel around for some pliers or a screwdriver."

Edna fidgeted, running her hand along the trunk's interior. "I can't find anything."

"Check your bra. You seem to have everything else in there."

Edna huffed. "I said my brassiere is like a purse, not a hardware store."

Charlotte shifted, throwing her leg over Maggie's thigh. "I've got an idea. I'm wearing four-inch spike heels. If you can pull one off, I'll bet you could use it to knock out the reflector."

"Good thinking. Maybe you're not such a dumb blonde." Edna bent her arm backwards. "Try to lift your foot up to my hand, and I'll pull your shoe off."

Charlotte hiked her leg up toward Edna's outstretched hand.

Maggie tilted her head, using the phone as a light, and gave them instructions as if she were a game show host. "Charlotte, lift your leg two inches higher. Edna, move your hand a little to the left. No, your other left."

Edna closed her hand over the shoe and yanked. "Got it!" She brought the shoe up and used the spiked heel to whack at the red plastic covering of the brake light.

"Be careful. Those are expensive shoes." Maggie still didn't like the woman in the trunk with her, but she hated to see a great pair of shoes get ruined.

"It's fine. I don't care," Charlotte said from behind her. "She can mangle that shoe all she wants. As long as it gets us out of here."

Maggie jumped as the elevator music stopped, and Mac's voice came over the phone. "Officer McCarthy here. How can I help you?"

The three women all spoke at once, crying for help and giving him instructions.

"Hello?" he asked. "Settle down. Who is this?"

Maggie shushed the other two women. "Mac, it's me, Maggie."

"Maggie? What's going on? Are you in trouble?"

Trouble was an understatement. "Yes. I'm with Edna and Charlotte Foster. We need your help. We've been kidnapped. We're trapped in the trunk of a car."

"All three of you are locked in a trunk? Together?"

Maggie rolled her eyes. "Yes. It's a big trunk, all right?"

"Okay. Take it easy. Is anyone hurt?"

Maggie was surprised at how much calmer she felt now that Mac's reassuring voice was on the other end of the phone. "No. I don't think so."

"Okay. Try to stay calm. Can you find anything in the car to knock out the reflector around the brake light? Can you try to kick it out?"

"We can't kick it out. As you can imagine, we're packed a little tight in here." Maggie knew it was no time for sarcasm, but geez. "Edna's whacking at it with a shoe."

"Good. Now, tell me what happened. Do you know who took you?"

Edna stopped hitting the reflector and hollered over her shoulder. "That little weasel Leonard!"

"Shh, Edna. We don't want him to hear us. Just keep working on that light." They could hear music pumping through the car speakers, so Maggie was fairly certain their voices would be masked, but she wasn't taking any chances. "Mac, it was Leonard. His car was parked in the garage by Jeremy's office. He had a gun and forced us into the trunk."

"All three of you?"

"No. Charlotte was already in here."

"This story just keeps getting better and better. Can you tell me anything about the car?"

"Yeah. We're in the trunk of a burgundy Mercury Marquis. It's an older model."

"Put out an All-Points Bulletin for it." Edna turned and called in to the phone. "If I only had my danged purse. I have the license plate written down in it. I think it has a seven in it. And a one."

Mac's sigh could be heard through the speaker. "You can thank Ms. Allen for her advice and then tell her that I've got this."

"She can hear you. It's on speaker."

A loud crack filled the trunk as the shoe heel cracked through the plastic and light spilled in through the broken reflector. Edna whooped in celebration. "I got it!"

"Can she see anything out of the hole?" Mac asked. "Anything to tell me where to find you?"

Edna wiggled her body, but couldn't get any traction to scoot up. "I can't get to it. I'm too danged short."

"Tell her to stick her hand out and wave it around. Maybe another car will see it and call it in. I'm heading to dispatch right now to see if any calls have come in. Maybe someone saw something in the parking garage and may know which way you were headed."

Edna grunted as she tried to push her hand through the reflector hole. "I can't get my whole hand through."

"Then just do the fingers. Anything to get another car's attention," Maggie told her. "Mac, she's trying now. Don't hang up."

"Don't worry. I'm not going anywhere. I won't leave you gals."

A lump filled Maggie's throat and tears filled her eyes. She knew they could count on the detective. "Thank you."

"Hey now. No crying. We've already had enough of that for one day. I'm still here." He chuckled. "It takes more than one failed pass at you to run me off."

Edna gasped. "He made a pass at you?"

"Oh, my gosh, Edna. Focus. Sadly, right now, you are our best hope at getting us out of here."

Maggie appreciated the cop's attempt to joke with her. Regardless of their earlier encounter, she knew he would do everything he could to find them. He was too good of a cop to let a little thing like a kiss get in the way of doing his job.

"Hey, we got something," Mac said excitedly. "Someone just called in to say they were behind an old car, and someone was sticking their hand out the back brake light and flipping them off. Wait. Flipping them off?"

"Edna, are you giving people the finger?"

"I told you I couldn't get my whole hand out there, and you said use your fingers." Edna cackled. "You told me to get their attention."

"You're doing fine, Edna." Mac's breathing sped up. "I'm running to my car now. The 911 operator is keeping them on the line, and she'll keep in contact with me through the radio. The caller said they were out on I-9, coming up to the bridge where you crashed into the lake."

Maggie's heart went into overdrive, beating wildly at the memory of their car plunging into the water. "What if Leonard's planning to finish us off by driving this car into the lake?" She knew how fast the car would fill with water. The thought of drowning while trapped in the trunk of the car had Maggie squirming and gasping for air.

"Maggie, it's okay." Charlotte spoke calmly behind her. "Leonard loves this car more than anything. He would never crash it into a lake."

That thought calmed Maggie a little. Plus, the thought of the blonde thinking of something she hadn't really irked her. She tried to control her breathing. Think. She had to calm down and think. "Of course. I know where he's taking us. He's going to Jeremy's."

The image of seeing Jeremy filled her heart. She wanted to tell him that she was sorry for not believing in him and not coming to him to talk it out in the first place. Hopefully, she would get that chance to talk to him. Who knew what Leonard's plans were once he got to Jeremy?

Mac spoke calmly from the speaker phone. "You're probably right, Maggie. I'm sending a squad car to Jeremy's place, and I'm headed that way now. If you are near the bridge, you're probably less than five minutes away. I need you to be prepared for when the car stops."

"Okay. What should we do?"

"I don't want to lose this line of communication with you. I need you keep the phone on speaker, and I'll mute my end so he won't hear me. You'll need to keep it somewhere on you so I can still hear what's going on. It has to be somewhere that Leonard won't notice. Can you hide it in a pocket or something?"

Maggie knew the perfect something to hide it in. "We'll put it back in Edna's bra."

"Oh-kay. I probably didn't need to know that, but there is a fairly good chance that Leonard will not search there."

"I'd say it's a hundred percent chance," Edna said. "Nobody messes with my goodies."

Maggie hoped she meant the trail mix and not her actual goodies. "Okay, as soon as we stop, we'll hide the phone and make sure it's pointed out toward Leonard. I'll try to let you know what's happening."

"Good girl," Mac said. "But, don't be too obvious. Remember, I'm a detective. I'm pretty good at figuring stuff out. Don't do anything that will alert him. I'm about ten minutes away, but I'll get there as soon as I can. Don't worry if you don't hear us. We're not using sirens because we don't want to alert him that we're on to him."

The car turned sharply, throwing the women against each other, then came to an abrupt halt. Maggie spoke quickly into the phone. "Mac, we just stopped. I'm passing the phone to Edna. Hurry!"

"I'll be there," he said, then the line went silent.

Maggie handed the phone to Edna who dumped it back down the front of her shirt. She heard the sound of a key inserted into the lock, then she was squinting into the sun as the trunk opened and filled the crowded space with light.

"Get out!" Leonard had the gun pointed at them.

Maggie sat up and tried to help Edna climb from the trunk, then gestured to Charlotte. "What about her?"

Charlotte pleaded with her coworker. "Leonard, please. Do *not* leave me in this trunk."

Leonard squinted at the blonde, as if he were really thinking through his response. "Fine. You can come in, too. Hurry up, though. I don't want the neighbors to see us."

Yeah, a man holding a gun on three women climbing out of a trunk just might raise suspicion.

Maggie scooted forward in the trunk, then turned to reach behind her. She pulled the blanket the rest of the way off Charlotte and gasped. The younger women's blouse was torn and bloodied. A purple bruise swelled under her eye and angry red welts encircled Charlotte's wrists where a thick rope was knotted around them. Maggie looked her nemesis in the eye. "I'm sorry this happened to you."

Charlotte's eyes filled with tears. "I'm sorry too. I'm so sorry. Nothing happened with Jeremy. He didn't even know I was in his bed. I snuck in to his house to wait for him. But he never wanted me. He always wanted you."

Maggie was stunned at the tearful confession. Jeremy hadn't cheated on her. He didn't even know the woman was in his bed.

"That's enough confession." Leonard leaned into the trunk and pulled Charlotte forward. He grabbed the loose piece of duct tape from the trunk floor and pushed it roughly back against Charlotte's mouth. "Get out of the trunk." Leonard yanked Maggie's arm and pulled her from the car.

She stumbled, her legs cramped from being in the trunk, and grabbed for Edna. Speaking directly into her breast, she loudly asked, "What are we doing at Jeremy's?"

"What do you think we're doing here?" Leonard jerked Charlotte up, pulling her from the trunk. He kept a tight hold on her arm as he motioned with the gun for Maggie and Edna to move forward. Charlotte still wore one shoe and limped alongside her captor. "We're gonna go see your boyfriend and end this once and for all. I'm tired of messing around. Jeremy needs to pay, and soon he'll be joining Jim."

They rang the bell like a misfit band of trick-or-treaters. Maggie could hear Chewie barking, and prayed that Jeremy was home.

She sucked in her breath when he answered the door, pulling it open with one hand and holding the mangy dog with his other.

He looked terrible. His hair was a tousled mess and his glasses were askew. He wore black and yellow Batman pajama pants and a wrinkled white t-shirt. By the various stains on the front of his shirt, he looked as if he had been wearing the same clothes for several days. Although Maggie wasn't sure how he was covered with food stains, because he looked like he had lost weight.

That was just great. Over the last week, since they broke up, she had plowed through four cartons of cookie dough ice cream and gained five pounds. He looked like he had been eating pizza and something brown, and he loses weight. Life was not fair.

Jeremy squinted at the group, as if he couldn't quite grasp that they were standing on his doorstep. "What the heck are you all doing here?"

Maggie watched his expressions change as he took in her presence, then Charlotte's bruised face and duct-taped mouth, then finally the gun that Leonard held in his hand.

Leonard kept a tight grip on Charlotte's arm and pointed the gun at Maggie's head. "Don't try anything, Superhero. Let's just all go in the house."

Jeremy stood back. "What are you doing? What's this all about, Leonard?"

Leonard hustled the women into the living room. He shoved Charlotte to the floor by Jeremy's desk and motioned for the other two women to join her.

Maggie and Edna huddled on the floor, Maggie's arm around the older woman's shoulder.

Edna shifted her bosom and spoke loudly. "Yeah, Leonard. Why don't you tell us what this is all about? And speak up, I'm an old lady, ya know. I can't always hear so good."

Oh, my gosh. Talk about subtle. Maggie watched Leonard look questioningly at Edna, then turn his attention back to Jeremy. Once his head turned, she reached up and pulled the tape from Charlotte's mouth. The tape was only loosely stuck to her face, but Maggie was sure it must have been hard to breathe through the sticky patch.

Charlotte sucked in air, then whispered, "Thanks."

Maggie was happy to help the woman, but her main focus was on Jeremy and what she could do to assist him.

He looked over at her, pain evident in his eyes. "Maggie, I'm so sorry. I've been trying to call you. Nothing happened with Charlotte, I swear."

She nodded in assurance. "I know. Charlotte told me."

Jeremy looked miserable. "I'm so sorry I got you into this mess. If anything happens to you, to any of you, I'll never forgive myself."

"It's okay, Jeremy. We're okay."

"All right. Enough of this lovey-dovey nonsense. Everyone needs to quit talking so I can think." Leonard rubbed his hand through his hair, leaving it sticking up in haphazard spikes. "None of this is going how I planned. I only wanted to take Charlotte. To take her away and make her fall in love with me again. If these two stupid bitches hadn't have been snooping around my car and heard her in the trunk, we would be gone by now. I never wanted any of this."

Confident now that the women were okay, Jeremy turned his attention back to their assailant. "What *do* you want, Len?"

"What do I want?" Leonard's eyes took on a crazed quality as he waved the gun around Jeremy's living room. "This. This is what I want. I want a fancy car and a house like this and a woman like that." He pointed the gun at Maggie and Charlotte. "And I had one, then you took her away."

Chewie growled at Leonard, and Jeremy pulled the dog closer to him. "I don't understand. I pay you a very good salary. You could buy a house. You could easily get a new car."

Leonard hung his head. "It's so hard. I had so much debt, and I have to pay for mother's debt, and I spent so much money on *her*." He pointed the gun at Charlotte. "I bought her clothes and shoes and jewelry. I loved her." He reached into his pocket and pulled out a square ring box. "I bought you this. I was going to ask you to marry me. I spent four thousand dollars on an engagement ring. For nothing." He threw the box violently across the room.

The game of fetch was too much for Chewie. He broke loose from Jeremy, running to sniff the box. Maggie quietly called him over and he ran to her, the tiny box in his mouth. She grabbed for his collar and pulled the big dog into her lap.

Holding the dog against her, she tightened her grip on his collar. The dog tags and the small Chewbacca head toy hanging from the collar swung against her hand. Maggie grabbed for the toy, and it popped open in her hand. She had never paid much attention to the action-figure head before, because she was usually trying to keep the giant mutt from slobbering on her.

Looking closer, she twisted the Chewbacca head in her hand. Holy zip drive! The little toy hanging from the dog's collar actually contained a hidden flash drive. She nudged Edna and nodded slightly to the toy in her hand. Edna's eyes widened, then cut to the desk behind them, in silent communication.

The three sat on the floor in front of Jeremy's desk. His monitor sat on top, bubbles floating around the screen. The computer sat under the desk, two empty USB ports on the front. If Maggie could just get a little closer, she could insert the flash drive. She fidgeted with the collar, trying to get the toy loose and slowly scoot closer to the computer.

Leonard appeared not to notice her movements, his full attention on Charlotte. He took a step toward her, his voice full of pain. "I loved you. And you used me.

You took everything I gave you, then dumped me and moved on to Jim." He swung the gun to point back at Jeremy. "And to him. All I wanted was for you to love me, to make a life with you. But, you still loved Jeremy. Even when he loved someone else. Even though you think he's a murderer."

Jeremy held his hands up in surrender. "I'm not a murderer. I didn't kill Jim. I didn't kill anyone. I don't even kill spiders. I put them outside."

"That's true," Edna said. "I've seen him do it."

Maggie kicked out a foot at Edna, shushing her so she wouldn't draw any unneeded attention to them. She had the *Star Wars* head free and gripped in her hand. She just needed a chance to slip it into one of the USB ports.

Charlotte spoke up for the first time. "What he's saying is true. I do love you, Jeremy. Working for you has changed my life. You're the reason I come to work in the morning. And I don't care what you did. I'll stand by you."

Jeremy stared at Charlotte in shock. "Charlotte, I didn't *do* anything. I did not murder Jim."

Charlotte shook her head, as if trying to digest this new information. "What do you mean, you didn't murder Jim? But I thought once you found out that he was selling the secrets of the new video game to Skyler, you killed him. That's why I lied and said you were with me the night of the murder. I gave you an alibi. I was trying to protect you. Jeremy, I still love you."

"I appreciate that, and I do care about you as a person, Charlotte, but I'm in love with Maggie." Jeremy still had his hands in the air. "And I didn't find out about Jim selling the game information until *after* he was murdered. So I had no reason to hurt him."

"But what about the emails and the money? I saw the threats you made to him."

"I didn't send those emails. Someone's been trying to make me look guilty, but I liked Jim. I gave him that money as a bonus for working so hard."

Leonard laughed. "You're such a patsy. You deserve to go to jail for this murder. You gave a guy a bonus that was stealing your code right out from under your nose. I worked twice as hard for you, and you never gave me a bonus."

Jeremy lowered his hands and his voice. He spoke calmly, as if talking to a small child. "I'm sorry about that, Leonard. I can see now that was a mistake on my part. But let's just talk about this. I'm sure we can work something out. Why don't you just put the gun down, and we can talk?"

"You must really think I'm an idiot," Leonard replied, a nasty sneer on his face. "That's the problem. You never saw my true potential. You felt sorry for me. Poor Leonard, so shy, always washing his hands, didn't talk to anybody. Well, that was the old Leonard."

He nodded at Charlotte. "She came along and changed all that. She saw me for how smart and funny I was. Or so I thought, until I found out she was just using me to buy her things and to get my input on the new game. Half the code she wrote for you on that fancy new game of yours, I came up with. Just so she and her new boyfriend could sell it to her good buddy, Skyler."

Edna gasped. "So, really Charlotte was the murderer all along." She pointed at the blonde, waving her arms and scooting in front of Maggie and the dog, blocking them from Leonard's view. "You just used these men and threw them away once you got what you wanted from them. How much did Skyler pay you to give him the secrets to the game? What was Jim's life worth? The price of a swanky car, a new pair of shoes?"

Charlotte shook her head. "I didn't kill Jim. I liked Jim. But, I love Jeremy. I've known Skyler for years, since high school. He tried to weasel information about the new game out of me, but I told him 'hell, no'."

"That's easy for you to say now." Edna raised her voice, speaking as if she were Jessica Fletcher and she had just solved the case. "But, you just admitted you had a relationship with Jeremy's biggest competitor. And we know you and Skyler were in Chemistry Club together. So, besides the fact that that makes you total nerds, it means you would know how to develop a poison to kill someone. Someone that you already used and just needed to get rid of. Leaving you free to either go back to Skyler or continue making money selling off secrets from Jeremy. It sounds to me like you had the means, the motive, and the opportunity."

"No way," Charlotte said. "Skyler knows my allegiance to Jeremy. He knows I would never turn on him. Besides, one night we were out drinking, and he let it slip that he didn't need me to get to the codes anymore. That he had an insider working at Rogers' Realms and was paying someone in our company to give him the codes."

"Who was it?" Jeremy asked.

"I didn't know. I thought it was Jim. He worked the closest with the game. So, I started dating him to keep an eye on what he was doing and to see if I could get him to admit that he was selling the information to SkyVision. Once I saw the proof of the payout and the threatening emails from you, I was sure that you had found out about Jim and taken care of him."

"Those emails were fake," Jeremy said. "I told you I never sent them. But how could you have seen *my* emails? Who showed you all this evidence?"

Charlotte lifted her bound hands and pointed at Leonard. "Him."

Before Leonard could speak, the voice of a ghost filled the room. While Edna was distracting them with her wild accusations, Maggie had inserted the flash drive. It had taken a minute to load, but now Jim's face filled the screen and thanks to Jeremy's surround sound, his voice could be heard clearly throughout the room. Maggie noticed Edna turn her chest toward a speaker and hoped Mac was still hearing all of this information.

"If you are watching this, then that means either something has happened to me or you have kidnapped my dog." Jim looked like he was in his office, speaking into the camera on his laptop. His whole face covered the screen. "And if that's the case, give him back, you sick bastard!"

Maggie felt Chewie pull away from her, watching Jim's face on the screen. The big dog tilted his head back and let out a mournful howl. Poor baby.

"I am making this video as proof that something rotten is going on in the Realm. I hope Jeremy gets to eventually see this. Jer, if you're watching, know that I was always faithful to you, dude. I was approached by Skyler Humphries from SkyVision about six months ago. He'd heard that we were developing this new software that was gonna change everything, and he wanted to pay me to give him the codes so he could launch the game before us. At first, I thought no way, then I realized that if I didn't say I'd work with him, then he would just go after someone else. And he was offering a *lot* of money, dude. So I kept stringing him along and giving him bits and pieces of code that were just a little off from what we were developing. He put a bunch of money in my account, but I never spent a dime of it, I swear."

The room was silent, all mesmerized by Jim's video confession.

The programmer continued his story. "Then SHE showed up. Man, I have never had a woman like Charlotte Foster pay any attention to me. I fell for her, and I fell hard. I wanted to believe in her, but I'm not a total dope. I knew that she had a connection to Skyler. They were old high school buddies or something. I felt like she wanted me to give the codes to her old friend and so I kept feeding him little clues, but never anything that would give him the real code that he needed to create the artificial intelligence in the new game. But I gotta tell ya, man. I was tempted. I *really* liked this girl. I mean, have you seen her? She's beautiful."

Maggie was surprised to see tears rolling down Charlotte's cheeks. Maybe she did have feelings for Jim after all.

"But then, after so many false leads, I think Skyler started to get suspicious. I found out that he was working with someone else in the company. I started doing a little digging. Hacking into the other employees' accounts. Sorry, Jer, but you need better security. Especially when you hire a bunch of brainy tech guys. It was cake for me to break the code and see the real guy that Skyler was working with. And he was giving him the *real* information. I was online when he sent out a file with the string of code that told SkyVision how to develop the new system. Thank goodness I saw it when I did. I intercepted the file and replaced it with a fake one. But, man, was I surprised when I saw who the real company spy was."

The room held their collective breath as they waited for Jim to name the real culprit.

Jim smiled into the camera, shaking his head. "I couldn't believe it. That little nerdy guy, Leonard. I totally didn't think he had it in him."

"Turn that off. Now." Leonard's voice held a note of barely controlled steel. "Who did that? It's all lies. He's lying."

Maggie had been studying Leonard as he watched the computer monitor. His full attention was on Jim's video. The gun hung limply from his hand.

As a woman lawyer, Maggie thought it was important that she knew how to protect herself in case one of her clients wasn't happy with her. She had taken several self-defense classes and knew that she could take Leonard down if she went after him while he was distracted.

She watched his control slipping. His whole focus was on the screen. Now was her chance. She pushed off from the floor, lunging at him, her nails out, ready to kick and bite and scratch. Whatever it took to knock the gun loose.

Unfortunately, Leonard must have taken the same type of class. For a short, nerdy-looking guy, he was extremely fast, and she was surprised at his agility. He easily side-stepped her, bringing his arm back and backhanding her across the side of the head with the heavy gun.

The metal hit the side of her forehead and pain exploded in Maggie's skull. She fell to her knees, clutching her head and crying out in pain. Chewie ran to her side, licking at her head. She blinked and looked up at Jeremy.

Seeing Leonard hit her must have been more than he could take, because in the next instant, Jeremy launched himself at the smaller man.

Maggie watched Jeremy run at Leonard, his arms outstretched, ready to tackle him.

The sound of the gunshot shattered the air. Maggie watched in horror as Jeremy staggered back. Clutching his stomach, a burst of bright red blood blossomed on his white t-shirt beneath his hands. She heard a woman scream and wasn't sure if it was Charlotte or herself.

Oh. My. Gosh. How could Jeremy have been shot? This could not be happening.

Leonard stood in the middle of the living room, a look of shock on his face. He held the gun outstretched in his hand while he yelled at Jeremy. "Now, look what you made me do! I just wanted to take Charlotte away. I didn't care about your stupid game and the rivalry between you and SkyVision! It was idiotic! All I knew was I needed to get Charlotte away from you and Jim. Jim was easy. I laced his coffee cup with a homemade poison the night before I left the office. All he had to do was fill it with coffee and have a few sips. And if I could make Jeremy take the fall for his murder, then both of them would be out of our lives. It was so simple."

He looked pleadingly at Charlotte. "Don't you see? I did this all for you." He stared at the computer screen, Jim's picture still frozen on it, and waved the gun at Edna. "Turn that off! I don't even want to see his face."

Edna whimpered. "I don't know how. You have to do it."

"Oh, for the love of Pete. You are such a stupid old woman!" He strode forward, leaning over to stab at the power button.

Maggie was awed by the lightning speed at which Edna moved. Those classes at the Y must really be helping.

Edna's fist came up, connecting with Leonard's crotch, and a crackling sizzle sound filled the room, followed by the smell of burnt electricity. The gun dropped from Leonard's hand, and Edna kicked it away. Seconds later, he crumpled to the floor, a gurgling sound coming from his throat, still clutching his groin.

Edna tipped her head down and yelled into her bra. "Get in here, Mac. He's on the floor. I just stunned him in the crotch with my Taser."

Pushing up from the floor, Edna stood over Leonard. She pulled back her foot and kicked him in the ribs. "Who's a stupid old woman now, bitch?"

The next moment, the front door burst open, and policeman swarmed in, guns drawn and yelling orders. A young officer in a flack vest ran to Leonard, who was still lying on the floor, doubled over in pain. He cried out as the officer flipped him over and slapped handcuffs on his wrists.

Then Mac was there. He reached for Maggie, asking her if she was okay.

But Maggie only had one place she wanted to be. She crawled forward, screaming for someone to call an ambulance. To get Jeremy some help.

She wanted to fling herself into his arms but was afraid to touch him. Afraid to hurt him. Tears coursed down her cheeks as she knelt over him, grasping his hand. "Jeremy, I'm so sorry. Please forgive me. I should have believed you. I should have trusted you."

Jeremy squeezed her hand. "It's okay, Maggie. I understand. We both made mistakes. I just about died when I saw him hit you. I'm sorry I didn't protect you."

She didn't care about that. As long as he didn't die now. She heard Mac give the all clear, and there must have been an ambulance outside, because two paramedics rushed in. They pushed her aside and lifted Jeremy onto a stretcher and within moments he was gone.

Edna knelt beside her, taking her hand. "Come on, we can follow them to the hospital."

Maggie looked down at the older woman. "Edna, you are amazing. How did you do that?"

"I knew I had my portable mini-Taser with me. I always carry it in my bra, just in case I get mugged. I like to be prepared. I just had to bide my time and wait for my chance to use it when I knew I could for sure get the little bastard. I didn't want to waste my chance or risk having him take it away from me."

"You and your bra. You ought to add pockets and patent that thing." Maggie pulled Edna to her in a one-armed hug. "Come on, let's go to the hospital."

She stood up, gingerly touching her head. The hair on her forehead was matted and sticky with blood. The room spun, and she reached out to steady herself.

Mac's strong hand gripped her arm, steadying her. "Whoa there. Maggie, you're hurt. You need to get to the hospital."

Maggie nodded. Which was a bad idea, as it caused stars to fill her vision. "We were just saying that. But we don't have a car."

"We do." Sunny and Cassie rushed into the room, followed by Jake and Piper. They threw their arms around Maggie and Edna, crying and both talking at once. "We were so scared. Are you girls okay? Oh my gosh, you're bleeding."

Mac held up his hand, quieting the ruckus. "They can tell you about it later. Right now, I need you to drive them to the hospital to get checked out."

Jake smiled at Maggie. "I'll stay here and take care of Jeremy's place and keep an eye on the dog."

The dog. That beautiful, mangy mutt that had the evidence around his neck this whole time. Who would have thought?

"Thanks, Jake." Maggie put her arm around Cassie's shoulder and headed for the van. Sunny and Piper helped Edna, holding her arms and getting her secured in the car.

"We need to get you to the hospital right away. That wound is still bleeding." Cassie pulled open the back door and gingerly helped Maggie into the seat. "Don't worry. I'll drive fast."

Maggie had no doubt of Cassie's driving skills, having been in the car with her when they were late for a soccer game. She was happy to have Cassie break every speed limit in town today if it would get her to Jeremy quicker. "I'm not worried about me. A few stitches and some aspirin, and I'll be fine. I'm worried about Jeremy. He's the one who was shot."

Sunny reached forward and rested her hand on Maggie's shoulder. "He's tough. He's gonna be okay."

Maggie squeezed her friend's hand, afraid to speak for fear she would start crying. He *had* to be okay.

Six and a half minutes later, Cassie's van pulled into the emergency room parking lot. Sunny opened the door and reached to help Maggie out of the car.

Maggie waved her away. "I'm fine. Help Edna. I'll meet you in there."

Maggie set off across the parking lot, bursting into the emergency room and charging up to the desk. Every step she took set off an explosion of pain in her head, but she didn't care. She had to make sure that Jeremy was all right.

Pleasant Valley was a small town, and the emergency room waiting area was practically empty. One lone mother stood swaying in front of the television, a toddler asleep on her shoulder. An older nurse wearing blue scrubs sat at the emergency room desk, her gray hair pulled back into a tight bun. She looked up at Maggie as she charged the nurses' desk.

"I need to check on my boyfriend. His name is Jeremy Rogers. He was just brought in about ten minutes ago, and he'd been shot." A cool hand slid into Maggie's and grasped it firmly. Maggie was surprised to see Sunny next to her, but she held her hand tightly, thankful to have her friend near, praying the nurse would say something reassuring.

The nurse looked Maggie over, unfazed and clearly used to the drama of the emergency room. "You realize you're bleeding. We need to get your head checked out."

"Fine. I'll see a doctor about my head. But first, I need to know about Jeremy Rogers. Is he okay?"

The nurse paused a beat, her lips pursed as if she were deciding how much information to tell this crazy woman who was bleeding on her counter. "They brought him in a few minutes ago and took him directly into surgery. I can't tell you much else, but he was unconscious when they wheeled him by me."

Maggie's legs gave way, but Sunny caught her before she hit the floor.

The nurse yelled for some assistance, and a young man in scrubs appeared with a stretcher. He gently lifted Maggie onto it and wheeled her into an open examining room.

Sunny followed along, never letting go of Maggie's hand. "You're gonna be fine, Mags. Just try to relax."

Relax? How could she relax when the man that she loved could be fighting for his life in the operating room? Had she told him that she still loved him? What if he died before she got a chance to tell him how she really felt? That she needed him and wanted to be with him.

The guy in scrubs pulled on a pair of gloves and drew back Maggie's hair to examine her wound. "Looks like you're going to need a few stitches." He held a flashlight up and tested her vision and pupil dilation.

Maggie pushed against him, straining to sit up. "I'll just wait for the doctor. I really need to check on my boyfriend." Only a few weeks ago, she had cringed at the term "boyfriend", and now she was throwing it around like a Wiffleball.

"Ma'am, I am the doctor."

Maggie raised her eyebrows at the young man in scrubs. He did have a stethoscope around his neck. "You look way too young to be a doctor." She pushed up an inch and the room seemed to spin. Maybe she would lie down. Just for a minute.

The doctor laughed and pulled bandages and a syringe from the cart next to the stretcher. "Yeah. I get that a lot. I promise I'm old enough. I just have a baby face."

He reached for the antiseptic, but before he could begin to even clean the wound, the examining room curtain was yanked open. Cassie, Piper, and Edna filled the small room.

Cassie rushed to Maggie's side, pushing the doctor out of the way so she could check on Maggie's head. "How are you feeling? Are you doing okay?"

Maggie looked around in dismay at the crowded room. "How did you all get back here? I can't believe that nurse let you past her."

"Who, Marge? That old battle-axe?! I'm not afraid of her." Edna waved toward the emergency room entrance. "We actually went to high school together. Believe it or not, we were on the cheerleading squad together." Edna clapped her hands together and started a cheer. "Rah! Rah! Rah! Kick 'em in the jaw!"

Maggie held up her hand. "Stop! You're hurting my head! And my brain. I don't ever want to picture you, or Nurse Marge, in a cheerleading uniform."

"Oops. You're right. Sorry about that. Got caught up in the memory." Edna poked her head out of the curtain and yelled down the hallway. "Can we get a doctor in here? My friend is bleeding."

Cassie turned to the man in scrubs and smiled sweetly. "Sorry about my friend, she left her manners in her other purse." Or in Edna's case, her other bra. "Can you help us find a doctor?"

He sighed. "I *am* a doctor."

Edna laughed. "Good try, buttercup. Now, why don't you run along back to high school and help us get a real doctor in here."

"I am a *real* doctor." He waved his stethoscope in the air. "Now, if you'll excuse me, I need to administer some stitches to your friend here."

Edna held up her hands. "All right, all right. You're a real doctor. You don't have to get all touchy about it."

"Yeah, he gets that a lot," Sunny explained.

"It's his baby face," Maggie added. She lay still as the baby-faced doctor cleaned her wound. "So, um, doctor, can you please tell me if you know anything about Jeremy Rogers? He was brought in a little bit ago with a gun-shot wound."

He shook his head. "I don't know much. I know he's in surgery with Dr. Holliday, and I'm sure he'll take good care of him."

"Dr. Holliday? The veterinarian? He's a people doctor too?"

The doctor chuckled. "No, the veterinarian is Dr. Holliday's brother. I assure you the man operating on your boyfriend is a *real* surgeon."

Geez. Small towns.

An hour later, the Pleasant Valley Page Turners sat in the family waiting room, anxiously anticipating the arrival of the surgeon with news about Jeremy.

Sunny had called Jake to update him. He was still at Jeremy's, dog-sitting and waiting for the police to finish clearing the scene. He reported that Chewie seemed fine after the recent drama and had since eaten a coaster and half a throw pillow.

Drew and Dylan had shown up with a pair of yoga pants and a t-shirt for their mom so she could change out of her blood-stained clothes. She now sat between Sunny and Cassie, her face scrubbed clean of makeup and a white bandage on her forehead.

Dr. Baby-face had given her some ibuprofen and instructions to take it easy for a few days, but an otherwise clean bill of health. She nervously tapped her fingernail against the wooden arm of the chair, noting a chip in the polish. She would take it easy when she knew Jeremy was okay.

Maggie sighed in frustration. "I just wish Dr. Holliday would come out and tell us something already."

Drew leaned over and whispered to Piper. "Why is she waiting for the veterinarian?"

Piper shushed him. "The veterinarian is his brother. Dr. Holliday is the one working on Jeremy."

The door of the waiting room opened, and the surgeon entered. All the members of the book club and Maggie's sons stood up to hear the news.

Why they all stood up was a mystery. Maybe because when you get bad news, you're supposed to sit down. If Maggie were standing, it was one more safeguard that the doctor would only deliver good news.

The doctor cleared his throat. "Good evening. I'm Dr. Holliday."

Maggie held her breath, hanging on the doctor's next words.

"And your friend, Jeremy, is going to be fine."

The room released a cheer of joy, and Maggie sank into the chair, holding her hand to her mouth and letting out a sob.

The doctor continued: "The bullet went clear through and narrowly missed any vital organs. We had to open him up to determine if there was any internal bleeding. He's going to be in some pain and needs to stay in the hospital for the next several days, but barring any unforeseen complications, he should make a full recovery."

Maggie stood to shake the doctor's hand. "Thank you so much. We really appreciate everything you did for him. When can I see him?"

"They've moved him to a recovery room on the second floor. It will be awhile before he wakes up, but you can sit with him until he does." The doctor looked around the room full of people. "But only one at a time for now."

Sunny pulled Maggie into a hug. "I told you he'd be fine. I've been telling you for years that if you'd just listen to me, I'm always right." She smiled at her friend. "You go on up. We'll be down here when you need us."

Maggie hugged her. All she wanted right now was to be there for Jeremy when he needed her.

A door slammed down the hall from the hospital room, and Maggie jumped. She had been sitting in the chair next to Jeremy's bed for the last hour, holding his hand and watching him sleep.

Jeremy's eyes fluttered open, and he looked around the room. "Maggie?"

She leaned forward, hesitantly touching his shoulder. "Hey, Jeremy. I'm here."

He took a deep breath and his eyes cut to the bandage on her forehead. "Are you okay?"

Leave it to Jeremy to take a bullet and then ask if she was okay. She smiled reassuringly. "Yes, I'm fine. Couple of stitches is all."

"And Edna and Charlotte? Are they okay?"

Maggie nodded. "Edna's fine. She's in the best shape of all of us. They brought Charlotte down here and treated her for abrasions. She was pretty bruised up and a little dehydrated from being in the trunk all day. They gave her some fluids and bandaged her wrists and released her several hours ago. She said something about spending the rest of the night soaking in a bathtub with a book."

Jeremy smiled. "That sounds like her. She loves to read. Maybe you guys could ask her to join your book club."

Maggie gave him a look.

He grinned. "Too soon?"

"Not if you want to get shot again."

Jeremy laughed, then held his side. "Wow. That really hurts." He looked down at his bandages. "I know I'm supposed to be a big, tough guy and all that, but holy crap! That is some serious pain."

Maggie poured him a glass of water and handed it to him. "Is there anything I can do for you?"

"Don't ever leave me again." His voice was soft and sincere, all kidding set aside.

Tears filled Maggie's eyes as she looked down at him. She shook her head. "I won't. I should have stayed that day. I should have given you a chance to explain. I should have trusted you."

He reached for her hand, his voice thick with emotion. "Maggie, I create mind games for a living, but I don't play them. Especially with you. This gunshot hurts, but it's nothing compared to the pain of losing you. It broke my heart when I thought I'd lost you."

Tears fell freely down her cheeks. "You didn't lose me. I'm right here. And I'm not going anywhere."

He reached up to touch her cheek, wiping away her tears. "Maggie, you mean everything to me. I am completely, madly, crazy in love with you."

Maggie swallowed and squeezed his hand. "I love you, too, Jeremy." She leaned down and laid a kiss gently on his lips.

His hand came up and fisted in her hair, dragging her mouth deeper against his. She kissed him back, fiercely and with all the emotion she could pour into one kiss.

He groaned, and she pulled back. "I'm sorry. I don't want to hurt you. I don't want to ever hurt you again. I still can't believe you were shot."

Jeremy smiled and waved his hand. "Ahh, this is nothing. It's just a flesh wound." He winked at her. "Besides, I heard that chicks dig guys with scars."

It was a crisp Sunday morning. Maggie and Jeremy sat on her deck, enjoying a cup of coffee. It had been two weeks since the shooting, and the feel of fall was in the air.

Maggie pulled the plaid blanket tighter across their laps. She heard the tap of toenails and looked up to see Barney step out on the deck and give a bewildered look to the giant dog that was lying in his bed.

Actually, it was more like Chewie was lying *on* the bed, since his big body completely engulfed the smaller dog's cushion. Barney tentatively pawed at Chewie, emitting a little whine, then curled up against the larger dog's side, resting his head on his paws.

"Aww, aren't they sweet?" Maggie tilted her face up to Jeremy's. "Have you decided if you're keeping him or not?"

Jeremy chuckled. "Oh, I think that was decided the first day I brought him home. I've never seen myself as a dog person before, but now I really like having the big guy around. When he isn't eating my household furnishings, he's quite good company. And he amuses me."

Maggie grinned. "I knew you were keeping him." Her voice took on a more serious tone. "And how about the other one? Are you keeping *her*?"

Jeremy raised an eyebrow. "I'm guessing you mean Charlotte?"

Maggie nodded.

"She has agreed to stay on through the launch of the new system, but she is looking for another job. She's expressed interest in moving to Seattle, and I told her I would give her a recommendation and do what I could to place her in another company."

"That's nice of you."

"I'm a nice guy."

Maggie looked into Jeremy's eyes. He *was* a nice guy. And he was *her* nice guy. After the last few weeks, she was certain that Jeremy was the man for her. He really was someone she could trust.

Maggie had taken the last few weeks off work to be with Jeremy. She wanted to take care of him, bring him soup, and plump up his pillows. Whatever he needed, she wanted to provide.

They had spent hours talking, laughing and sometimes crying. But they had passed their time *together* and she knew that with him was where she wanted to be.

If falling in love was one of life's games, she finally felt ready to get back on the field and participate again. Whether they were tossing a basketball on the court or immersed in a battle in a virtual world of computer characters, she knew she wanted Jeremy on her team.

On her team. As her partner. Having Jeremy by her side, she now saw her future with him as a game she couldn't wait to play.

The End

OTHER BOOKS BY JENNIE MARTS

Coming in 2014
Just Another Maniac Monday
Book 3 in the Page Turners Series

Another Saturday Night and I Ain't Got No Body
Book 1 of the Page Turners Series
On Amazon: http://amzn.com/B00AQPJ924
On Amazon UK:
http://www.amazon.co.uk/dp/B00AQPJ924

Be the first to find out when the newest Page Turners
Novel is releasing and hear all the latest news and
updates happening with the Pleasant Valley Page
Turners Book Club by signing up for the newsletter at:
jenniemarts.com

If you enjoyed this book, please consider leaving a
review!

ACKNOWLEDGEMENT

There are so many people involved in producing a book and each one deserves my thanks.

First and foremost, I must thank my husband, Todd, for always supporting me and his consistent belief in my success. His steadfast love and strength keeps me going and I appreciate every night that he's walked into the house and found me bent over my laptop, still in my pajamas and kindly offered to make supper. I owe my sons, Tyler and Nick, my gratitude for always listening to new plot ideas and marketing strategies and for making all of their friends purchase my books.

I have so many wonderful women who give up their time and expertise to proofread and edit my books. My undying thanks go out to: Linda Kay, Joelle Whinnery, Terry Gregson, Jean Slane, Lee Cumba, Julie Feuerbach and Carla Albers.

I have been blessed with an amazing group of writers who support each other and offer me their opinions and encouragement. My thanks go out to Lana Williams, Anne Eliot, Cindi Madsen, Marla Bell, the Pikes Peak Romance Writers, and the Colorado Indie Authors. Special thanks goes out to Michelle Major who has offered me countless hours of advice, encouragement, accountability, and a friendship that means the world to me.

Thanks to Arran McNicol of Editing 720 for his superb editing skills.

Finally, my books would not be complete without the incredible work done by The Killion Group on my covers and formatting. Thanks so much to Kim Killion and Jennifer Jakes for their advice, their fast and efficient work and their incredible creative talents that make my covers and marketing material look amazing. You girls rock!

AUTHOR BIO

Jennie Marts loves to make readers laugh as she weaves stories filled with love, friendship and intrigue. She's the author of the Kindle Bestselling romantic comedy, Another Saturday Night and I Ain't Got No Body. Reviewers call her book "laugh out loud" funny and full of great characters that are "endearing and relatable."

She writes from the mountains of Colorado where she lives with her husband, two sons, a parakeet, and a golden retriever named Cooper. Jennie enjoys being a member of (RWA) Romance Writers of America, the Pikes Peak Chapter of RWA, and Pikes Peak Writers.

Jennie is addicted to Diet Coke and adores Cheetos. She loves playing volleyball and believes you can't have too many books, shoes or friends.

Jennie loves to hear from readers. Follow her on Facebook at <u>Jennie Marts Books</u> or Twitter at @JennieMarts.

Visit her at www.jenniemarts.com and subscribe to her newsletter for the latest on new releases and to find out the current happenings with the Pleasant Valley Page Turners.

Made in the USA
Lexington, KY
17 January 2014